Publishing
With
InDesign

3rd Edition

Publishing
With
InDesign

3rd EDITION COVERING ADOBE INDESIGN CS5®
INTERMEDIATE & ADVANCED TRAINING

Gaining Control with
Practical Production Skills

A Training Publication of

These materials were written & designed by
David Bergsland ©2001;
edited, expanded, & formatted
by David Bergsland ©2010
Radiqx Press • All rights reserved
ISBN# 978-0-557-36451-0
This book is distributed and the ISBN# provided by Lulu
http://www.radiqx.com •
chakham@radiqx.com

This book is dedicated to my wife, Pastor Patricia, & daughter, Elizabeth.

Without their love & support I'd still remain the same crazy, nasty hippie I was in the mid 1970s when I met the two of them while Pat was just beginning her seminary studies. Of course, Elizabeth was only four then but she changed my life as surely as her mother did.

I couldn't do what I do without the love they taught me.

The original 1st edition foreword (2000)

It's been a wonderful ride. About six years ago, a sales rep from Delmar called me on the phone in my lab where I taught Commercial Printing at Albuquerque TVI. She wanted to know if I was using any of her books. I explained that I couldn't because they were all application-specific and I taught all the major software at the same time in the same lab. As a result, I was forced to write all of my own materials. I had to create everything from scratch because nothing existed that taught the basic principles of the paradigm shift our industry was undergoing.

She said, "You interested in writing a book?"

Like an idiot, I said, "Sure!"

About a month later I received a call from an editor from Delmar, in Albany, N.Y.. He asked me if I was serious about that book.

Again, in blissful ignorance, I said, "Sure!" I explained that I was a nobody who just liked to write. I told him that I needed a conversational book, in the style of my lectures, or the students would refuse to read it. Actually, we talked for about forty-five minutes.

The result was that he told me they were receiving proposals on a book like this and he'd like to see one from me.

That time around

That first book was a revelation. What I discovered was a paradigm shift. All of the rules that worked when I was in industry were changing faster than anyone could write them — except for in the magazines. One of the advantages of a paradigm shift is that the new persons start on the same footing as the old hands. Everyone has new rules. Often, in fact, the new people are not hindered by the habitual reactions from the old paradigm.

My sources were *MacWorld, MacUser, Publish, Step by Step* (both), NADTP, GATF, NAPL, *Graphic Arts Monthly, American Printer, Southwest Graphics, Aldus* (now *Adobe*), and several others. The best was and is *Before & After* by John McWade. Here I found a man after my own heart ... and look at what he is doing!

There were no textbooks on this new trail. I used Roger Black's *Desktop Design Power* and Robin Williams's books. These two authors are probably my biggest influences. They had a conversational tone that I liked – clear, concise, and entertaining *PLUS* my students would actually read it. The old printing textbooks were never used at all. I needed a retail book, but none of the well-written computer books covered printing problems adequately or even accurately.

The advantage of being forced to start from scratch became obvious. Not being hampered by traditional ways of doing things, I developed an entirely new method of instruction. Based on my twenty-plus years in the industry, I knew what employers needed. I discovered that students also thrive when they are taught real-world solutions to real-world problems.

This time around

This textbook is written as an entertaining read. It is meant to be conversational and a little controversial. My primary concern is the higher learning skills – we need graduates who can think and solve problems. This means asking difficult questions.

This book is quite different from the first book in that it actually teaches software. It is different from my second book in that it assumes much more advanced knowledge. This third book contains a lot of review materials for those who do not have comprehensive training. But it is primarily directed to advanced students and people with prior publishing knowledge obtained through informal training or simple work experience.

Going online

In 1996, it became obvious that most industry communications were going to be over the Net. As a result of that, I converted all of my course-work to online instruction. At present, all of my students have the option to do all or part of their work online. This is a real boon for students who are convinced that they can survive professionally on a PC (my lab is all Mac). More than that, it has enabled employed personnel to upgrade their skills while working. What I saw in 1996 has become fact. For this book, all communication with the publisher has been via email, the final digital documents will be PDFs FTPed to the printer in Canada, and everything is moved around attached to emails.

My goal is extremely practical. What do you need to succeed in this industry? I am relentless about that. I call it reality orientation. That's what this book is all about.

David – June 1, 2000

PS: For those of you compulsive about these things, except for illustrations taken from *Printing in a Digital World*, I created everything. I wrote all the copy, shot or own all the photos, and drew all the drawings on my iMac, 96 MB RAM, 6 GB hard drive, plus a ZIP, JAZ, APS 4x4x20 CD-RW, and an Epson 636 scanner. My word processor is Mariner Write. My illustrations were done in FreeHand 9. The bitmaps were done in Photoshop 5.5. Everything was assembled in InDesign 1.5, from which I directly exported the PDFs for printing. Finally, I designed all my own fonts for this book.

Comments on the second edition

We've kept the original concept though the equipment has changed a little & we're using CS4 (specifically, Creative Suite 4 Design Premium). This time we're using 20" aluminum iMacs with 4 GB RAM, a 320 GB hard drive, an old Epson 4870 Photo scanner, Superdrive, and doing all the writing directly in InDesign.

Comments on the third edition

We've added coverage of new features from InDesign CS5 that apply to this book. Plus quite a bit was rewritten and cleaned up.

List of Contents

This book is a revised 3rd edition of Radiqx' 2nd edition from 2009 of my first book for InDesign 1.5 written in 1999-2000 and published by OnWord Press in the summer of 2000. That book was amazing in its arrogance and ignorance. My hope is that this one will be much more useful.

The book design

This is not a beautiful, clean, and elegant bit of classic typography. Of course you could see that at a glance at this two-page spread. Typography for a techniques book like this one is, of necessity, filled with styles to the point where they get busy and very complex.

This complexity serves our purposes very well. We need to be able to show you hundreds of different options. We need to stretch your mind to see some possibilities that you may not have even seen before —ones you may not have thought possible. For example, we have used optically aligned paragraphs and discretionary ligatures throughout. This is partly because we really like them and partly because you need to realize that we are not in the last millennium any more. They are one of the many advantages of OpenType Pro fonts (which we use almost exclusively).

In general everything is done with type except for the obviously placed graphics. If there is any doubt, we will attempt to remember to mention exceptions. But don't hold us to that, please. Our goal is one text frame per page, plus anchored graphics in the sidebar area as needed. (For example, the gradient square on the right margin in the next paragraph is a paragraph rule before paragraph added automatically with the paragraph style for our third level of heads–8-subhead 2. More about that later...)

This is an intermediate to advanced book

Assumptions: We have to set some basic ground rules for the typical reader that may or may not apply to you personally. Here are some of them:

- ⊕ **That you have the software:** You'll need InDesign. We're assuming that you have a Design Premium Creative Suite CS3, CS4, CS5, or newer.

- ⊕ **Desktop publishing:** We need to assume that you know a bit about publishing in general. You need to understand from the outset that experience with Office or other word processors will usually have to be tossed and often reversed to be usable

- ⊕ **Text editing skills:** We'll mention shortcuts, but other than that we'll assume this is an already acquired skill set.

- ⊕ **Tabs:** We also need to assume that you at least know that tabs exist & that you have at least attempted to use them before.

- ⊕ **Mac or PC:** We have to assume some of both. Captures will be Mac but the same capabilities are available on the PC & are usually called the same thing. The main thing to remember is that you will need 4 GB RAM minimum to use CS5 well. Plus for CS5 you need an Intel CPU.

- ⊕ **Illustrator and Photoshop skills:** We have to assume that you know how to use the Pen tool well and that you are reasonably fluent with Photoshop.

Although we are covering abilities through CS5, many of these capabilities have been available since version 1. We will mention new CS5 abilities as they appear. But most of these techniques will work in CS3, CS2 and some even in CS & Version 2.

 The light bulb: This graphic is used to call your attention to tips and special techniques. If we remember, we'll mention how far back in the versions they were introduced. But we are working in CS4&5 and have no real way to go back and check.

Fonts: All fonts used in normal styles are from the Hackberry Font Foundry: Amico family, Acadami family, Aerle, & others. They are available at: http://www.hackberry-fonts.com plus MyFonts.com and fonts.com — it's been a fun rewrite. We hope it's a fun read and you learn a lot.

David

September 2009 & March 2010

New in CS5

Simplified object selection and editing

⊕ **Do almost everything with the selection tool**

Live Corner Effects.

⊕ **Adjust corners individually**

Easy grid placement.

⊕ **Generate grids with arrow keys:** while adding objects

Track text changes

⊕ **Only works in story editor**

Paragraphs that span and split columns

⊕ **Covered on pages 62–63**

All-new Layers panel

⊕ **Reconfiguring grouped objects:** simply drag objects from one group to another in the Layers panel

Document-installed fonts

⊕ **Automatically install packaged fonts**

Live captions

⊕ **Generate static or live captions automatically:** from image metadata.

Gap tool.

Multiple page sizes

⊕ **Page Selection tool**

Interactive documents and presentations

⊕ **Animation panel; Object States panel; Timing panel; Media panel; Preview panel:** New panels help you add rich media to Page layouts

Integrates with CS Review

⊕ **Excellent resource:** but it costs extra by subscription

InDesign CS5 pages to Flash CS5 with greater fidelity.

Publishing With InDesign

For some of you: This is a new great adventure, learning how to use well what is probably the most powerful page layout application. Some of you are looking to get your working procedures for typography and page layout under some kind of control. Some of you are simply looking for tips and tricks. There is something in this book for all of you.

We are assuming that you have the CS5 Design Premium applications. We will be assuming a normal workflow, using Illustrator, Photoshop, Dreamweaver, and Acrobat as well as InDesign. Adobe has created page layout software that is extremely powerful, remarkably intuitive, and immensely adaptable.

We've got a bit of history behind us

Here's a wee example of desktop publishing in its early days: The quality was stupendous with dried lambskin pages, 24 carat gold inks, fine paintings and exquisite calligraphy

They say everything is new: we're really just a lot faster, much cheaper, and usually a lot more tense about whole process.

Nothing is enough

The basic fact of publishing remains. No matter how good InDesign 7 is—and it is very good, we need a suite of programs to do what we do. We have to assume you have Photoshop, Acrobat, and Illustrator—and know how to use them (plus Dreamweaver). We cannot do without any of these. Of course we also have to deal with files from Office, so we assume you know how to use that also.

Even if we do not use them all, we will receive pieces of our documents on all of these programs plus QuarkXPress and FreeHand. Though it is true that InDesign can open and convert PageMaker 6.5 and Quark 3 & 4 files, documents from the newer versions of Quark are still a problem to us. All we can do is ask for the pieces to be sent to us or that they save the Quark files back to version 4.1. Markzware does sell a plug-in to convert Quark files that has a good reputation. It's a bit spendy (to use a Minnesotanism), but it'll convert almost any Quark file to InDesign with minimal loss.

This is advanced instruction for designers who understand the basics of page layout

This book assumes prior knowledge

As mentioned in the front matter, this book assumes that you have been either working in or studying print production for a little while. All of your training may well have been OJT (that *"you'll have to figure it out because there is no one else in this company that knows anything about it"* type of training). But even if you had formal education, it is unlikely that the curriculum covered the materials in this book very well. The practicalities are usually ignored in the ivory towers of academia.

InDesign, like Quark, requires advanced knowledge. Although we will cover basic reviews of all topics you need to know, we have to assume:

- **Knowledge of Word**
- **Experience with a professional page layout application:** like InDesign, Quark, or PageMaker
- **You have exported graphics:** from creation programs
- **You have imported them:** into page layout programs
- **You know basic file management techniques:** mouse usage, text editing, cut/copy/paste, and so forth
- **We won't mention basic computer literacy**

In other words, we expect you to have a basic working knowledge of your computer and how to use it. Our experience suggests that many (if not most) of you were poorly taught in these areas. In fact, it is quite possible that our euphemistically named *reviews* will be brand new knowledge for many of you. But we will cover those things as we go.

Please be careful using the term *desktop publishing*. That phrase has become problematic for many of us — having nostalgic meaning for those who remember Paul Brainard, Aldus software, and the early days; but so widely defined that it has almost reached non-meaning. Now, desktop publishing currently refers to what we call Office use. These office personnel spend most of their time with business correspondence and materials, but they are often called upon to do the monthly newsletter for the personnel or customers.

We are dealing with digital publishing, at a professional level, using the Creative Suite fluently to produce finished digital documents for professional output.

Quite possibly you are one of those "Office" people

If you are called upon to produce the monthly newsletter, start designing brochures, catalog pages, and so on — you'll almost immediately discover that Office can't cut it. It isn't designed to do professional work for printing or the Web. You are entering a new world.

This book will be a bit of a stretch for you.

⬦ **Publishing is very expensive:** You really need to understand the options to make good decisions.

⬦ **It is ridiculously complicated:** When you first get started, you have no idea how complex it is. Printing (& web design) are immensely complex projects.

⬦ **Inadequate software:** You cannot produce professional printed results using Office. Work produced with a word processor is not professionally typeset, because the software is not capable of it. Readers have trouble trusting the output because it is so obviously not professionally done. You cannot make professional Websites with Office either. There are simply too many capabilities that Word or WordPerfect do not have and the ones it does have are far too difficult to implement. Worse yet are Publisher and Front Page. We know the price was good (free with Office on the PC), but you don't even get what you pay for. If you are serious, you need a professional solution — InDesign (hopefully CS4 or better) using styles habitually.

⬦ **Inadequate hardware:** Though it is true with XP Pro or better you can do this stuff on a PC, the major problem is that the PCs commonly available in an office do not have the power, the memory, nor the storage capacity that is needed for these projects. A machine that cost you less than $500 cannot do it. It is easy to prove that Macs can out produce PCs in this field by three to one or better, but that is a fight we refuse to take on here (though, in fairness, we must mention that PCs with the same capabilities as Macs are usually quite a bit more expensive). Mainly you need a Core Duo or better (Mac or PC, they use the same chips now), 4 GB RAM or better [see sidebar], 120GB hard drive or better, an Ethernet network or better, a good quality monitor, and a PostScript printer.

CPUs & RAM needs

Every new version of the Creative Suite requires more. The RAM needs usually double and the next level of outdated CPU is often dropped.

CS3 required: 1 GB RAM and dropped support for G3s

CS4 required: 2 GB RAM and dropped support for G4s (barely G5s)

CS5 needs: 4 GB RAM and Intel Macs

CS6 will likely need 8 GB RAM

Beyond the obvious experience and hard/software issues, there are many things that you can only learn with experience. Our hope is to share some of this experience with you to lighten your learning curve. Much Of this has to do with the nature of printing.

Printing is not dead!

More than that it is not going to die. Obviously, its position of strength and dominance in the our marketing economy has radically changed. However, there are many things about printing that need to taken into consideration for any project you produce.

Printing itself has changed radically: Beginning in the early 1990s the printing industry has gone through an amazingly radical, fundamental shift in how it works. This book, for example, will be printed on-demand. This means our printing company will hold our digital artwork and print off individual copies as they are ordered. That was impossible in the 20th century in most cases because there simply were no digital presses that could handle it. Now those presses are common.

Here are some things you need to consider when designing digital documents

✤ **Always design for print:** One of the major issues is that you must always need to design all of your work at print quality standards. Why? The simple answer is that print is high resolution with excellent type & graphics and the Web is not. The more accurate answer is that print requires much higher quality and resolution (usually 300 dpi with CMYK or spot colors). On the other hand, the Web is 72 dpi and RGB or indexed color. It is very easy to downsample (dumb down) print graphics to Web levels. It is not even theoretically possible to take a low resolution Web graphic (72 dpi GIF, PNG, or JPEG image) and bring it up to print quality unless you can reduce it in size to 25% or less.

✤ **Vector content is a huge benefit:** We are not talking about doing everything in Illustrator. InDesign produces vector content exclusively [& often more easily]. While it is true that we normally have some raster art from Photoshop, we quickly learn that keeping things in vectors simplifies our work a great deal.

So, who cares? Print is dead & we're totally online...

If you are purely online you are an extremely rare breed. What do you do when you have to deal with the most common request of a Website, "Do you have a brochure or a PDF of this page?" Obviously, this varies a lot. However, even for those organizations completely focused on the Web: what do you do when your visitors want something they can hold in their hand or hang on their wall?

In truth, you will be working with a mix of both media & more.

Web or print quality:

This?

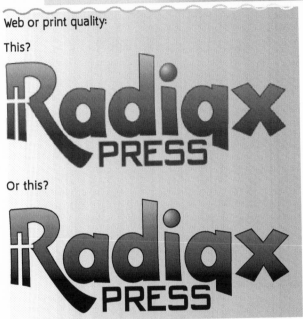

Or this?

For most situations it makes the most sense to start with print quality. The top graphic to the left looks very good on the Web. In print, it is horrible –pixilated & blurry. You can see the difference with the high resolution PDF just below the web graphic. Plus, there is the problem that the Web cannot do typography except in graphics. These graphics cannot be searched or edited easily. Much of our communication in publishing is influenced or even controlled by the quality of the typography, layout, and format. This is why most of the Web has been relegated to fulfillment & data. This is also why a great deal of office and in-house business output is not taken seriously. CSS can help the typography on the Web, but the media capabilities are simply not available for typographic excellence.

The bottom line: Print costs more, but it has much more impact when well done. There is no real replacement for print. We really do not see visitors to your sponsored event checking out the fancy interactive program on their cell or even your Website. If they do, they'll print out the program to bring along. The Web certainly has its place – especially in the Web 2 era. But you will be producing many printed projects for many varied reasons.

Print is not dead, but it is changing rapidly and radically

It is now just one of the many arrows in our quiver

So, how does this work in real life?

As you know, this industry has fully entered the digital age. All artwork is done digitally, proofed via email and online sessions, and delivered online. Wideband laptops, iPads, and smart phones are now commonplace. Only the largest files have to be FTPed now. Our dependence on FedEx is moving into the past. Almost all communication is over the web. Most fulfillment is online. This has become the norm far outside our small industry of graphic designers and page layout specialists.

This book is focused on publishing

We will be looking at multi-page documents: books, magazines, newsletters, catalogs, and so on. The techniques certainly apply to general graphic design, but our focus is a little different. However, we do recognize and use modern publishing venues which include on-demand printers like Lulu, Create Space, Zazzle, CafePress, and many others which do on-demand publishing of everything from books to skateboards and men's ties. (**NOTE:** *On-demand simply means that the piece is not printed until it is ordered and paid for.*)

In addition, you are commonly responsible for the graphics and page production of Web sites. Often, we are also responsible for simple multimedia in the form of simple interactive CDs and PDFs. Finally, because we are often the only artist in the place, we also produce all the graphics and set up the PDFs, HTML/CSS, and PowerPoint for presentations.

No wonder that there is no one program that will do it all. In fact, in some shops there is no one person who is allowed to do it all. So, before we can go on, we must discuss the things we do. I will try to mention most if not all the options.

 Please keep in mind: We offer many of these rather strongly stated opinions for several reasons. One is obviously to entertain. Another is to provoke discussion. A third is to give a hint of the wide variety of publishing solutions used in the industry. If you think we are wrong, good for you. *What is important is that you think.* Focus some of your time on software available, holes in your capabilities, and purchases you need to make. You need to do this regularly throughout your career.

You really must start with print quality
Let's discuss your options

Print first: Printing is very complex, as mentioned. When you start dealing with various printing companies, you will find an amazing and bewildering amount of options. Top-quality color offset printing is an extremely difficult craft. Bringing it in-house adds complexity beyond most capabilities unless you are very careful. Even black-and-white laser printers require a surprising amount of printing knowledge to use well.

Before we can talk about design we have to discuss output

You must know how you are going to produce your project before you start designing.

A lot of what is possible is controlled by the technology used by the company or printer you are going to use. Things like: what colors you can use, how large an area can you make solid color, how much ink can you pile on top of each other (known as ink limit in Photoshop), how thin can you make your lines, what fonts can you use, and much more.

The limitations are not good or bad — they just are. The printing technology restrictions are simply an integral part of the considerations for your design solutions.

Basic assumptions of professional output

PostScript or better: Professional publishing software was based on a page description language called PostScript—the current version of which is called Genuine Adobe® PostScript® 3. However, many of the features of the Creative Suites are dependent on transparency which PostScript does not support. There is now an option available called the *Adobe PDF Print Engine* that works directly with PDFs. This adds many benefits, such as the ability to support transparency [using PostScript requires flattening]. Always talk to your printing company or output supplier before you start designing to find out what the limitations and strengths are of your supplier. Mainly, it just involves a choice in your PDF settings when you export your final PDFs.

High resolution: Cheap printing uses 1200 dots per inch (dpi). Good quality printing normally uses 2400 dpi or more. No graphics produced by Office are more than 72 dpi (Web resolution).

Printable color: Printing is done with toner or ink. Full color uses CMYK — Cyan (turquoise blue), Magenta (a red that's closer to fuchsia), Yellow (an acidic yellow), and Black (a dark gray). Spot colors are custom mixed inks that print on their own plate (there are virtually no digital options for spot color printers). Office and the Web use RGB — Red, Green, & Blue. These are the colors of light and cannot be printed without a conversion to CMYK which causes massive color shifts and worse.

Pagination: Making booklets: this is the point where people become seduced by Publisher. But, Publisher doesn't even have the capabilities of Word — & yes, it is also 72 dpi and RGB color. The good news is that Markzware has a plug-in to convert Publisher files to InDesign called PUB2ID—Microsoft Publisher To Adobe InDesign. It costs a couple hundred dollars, but it is the only real solution.

Now we have enough background to move on to output. We'll leave the Web for another book. For now let's just talk about printing. Throughout your publishing career you will discover more and more about this fascinating craft. It (and the knowledge it requires) will form the basis of your professional competency.

Without printing and typographical knowledge, the best of your marketing efforts will fall flat.

Each type of printing has its own advantages.

There are 10 technologies, but only five are common

The first thing we have to discuss is the relative simplicity of the options. There are only six printing technologies in common use:

Lithography: Commonly called offset (often called traditional printing now) and used by commercial printers and many quickprinters. This is what most printing was in the 1980s and most of the 1990s. It is becoming a niche technology because of some of its limitations in short-run and makeready capabilities. It market strength is also severely compromised by the difficulty in finding press operators. Much of the excellent lithographic printing you see now is being done in Southeast Asia because of labor issues and other economic benefits of those economies.

Electrostatic: Commonly called digital printing and used by many quickprinters [AlphaGraphics, Sir Speedy, Minuteman Press, FedEx Office, and the like], copy shops, copiers, and laser printers. All of the toner-based digital presses are grouped under the general heading of electrostatic for our purposes. This technology now prints the majority of work especially in B&W work. (We know the color portion is growing at a phenomenal rate – though the various surveys give widely varying data that depends on how much in-house and office printing is included).

Stencil: This is usually called screen printing and used for clothing, bumper stickers, and the like. It's a sideline for most.

Inkjet: This is the most expensive type of printing and should be used only for large individual pieces like banners, billboards, large posters, trade shows, and booths. However, the latest Drupa showed some amazing new high speed, low cost inkjet technology. This is an area to watch. Some of the new inkjet presses are claiming 2,000+ impressions per minute. That comes very close to matching heat-set web offset printing.

Vinyl cutting: This is the technology now used by what used to be called sign painters. Real sign painters are almost completely extinct. Almost all signs are now cut vinyl or large inkjet prints.

There are five more that you need to be aware of.

Letterpress: This original printing technology is almost dead. But it is used for foil stamping and die-cutting and is often a sub-contracted portion of your major offset jobs. It does not play well with toner-based printing. It is commonly used for folders, awards, and invitations. In most cases, your printing supplier will guide you throughout the process.

 Don't forget about letterpress: Used well, the letterpress options can give your pieces great impact at little cost. For example, a single spot color plus foil is usually cheaper and can be much more elegant than full-color CMYK.]

Flexography is a variant of letterpress: It uses flexible rubber plates, is much cheaper than letterpress and is commonly used for packaging. You will need this if you sell prepackaged foods or products. Some people think this is more than 15% of all printing and its use is growing rapidly. Because of the flexibility of the plates, there are complicated geometric adjustments needed to print your shapes. You printing supplier can handle it with their software, but you will need to follow their instructions carefully.

Stencil 2: Digital mimeographs are also a stencil technology with many economic and speed advantages for non-profits and similar organizations, but they require printing knowledge to do well. They work like the old mimeographs, but at a much higher resolution, with faster printing speeds, and digitally made stencils. They had quickprint registration at best, but now there are 2-color and even 4-color presses. This is the only option for digital spot color, in most cases.

Engraving: Usually called gravure, this technology has always been very expensive to set up. It is very rare these days, but used for printing money. In most cases, use of this technology would be poor stewardship: beautiful but extravagant. However, for project with print runs in the millions, it really comes into it's own. There are new digitally imaged plate cylinders that might make gravure much more competitive with litho.

Dryography: A specialized technology used by top-end commercial printers that uses layered plates with the image burned through the top layer. You will not run across this unless you are printing large quantities of top-quality printing. However, at that level, it is very competitive with offset litho.

Every type of printing technology has its own benefits and limitations. Each has its own requirements. Each technology can do some things that the others cannot do. None are perfect. All have problems of some type. Your task will always be to design within those limitations. None of these different methods of printing is better or worse. They are different and each is the best choice in different specific circumstances. It is extremely important that you keep that in mind.

So, what are your choices?

Actually, we just listed them. You will use all of the five basic options, at least. But when would you want to use them? Let's go through the technologies in two basic categories: inhouse & outside supplier.

In-House: you own or lease the equipment

Non-professional: We use the common scenario of a secretary or receptionist with Office on a cheap PC printing on a cheap, non-PostScript

laser printer, inkjet, or copier as a bad, expensive example as we go through this book. If your organization fits this category, you need to make a major decision right now before you continue reading this book. Do you want or need to make your production more effective? Are you willing to invest time & money for personnel, training, & equipment to make professional production a reality for your work?

Office & A Copier

One thing not mentioned that needs to be covered— this "cheapest" setup is not the cheapest to use. You will waste a lot of money because of the limitations of this type of operation. You need to be thinking about the Creative Suite and a PostScript office-quality production printer. This option is readily available and assumed in this book.

None of the suggestions we are going to make will have any use within a production environment using Office on a cheap printer.

Minimal hardware & software

Computer: Seriously, you really need a Mac. But having said that, we realize that many of you, for various reasons will not do this. So: you need an Intel dual core chip, minimum; 4 GB RAM, minimum (8 GB recommended); and at least a 120 GB hard drive. Of course, it is hard to buy anything less now unless you are trying to pay less than $1000 (and that is like trying to buy a new car for under $10,000 – possible but not recommended, if you drive a lot).

Monitor: You need a good monitor, at least 17" but 19" or 20" is best, that can be color profiled. This will normally be an LCD, but a CRT will give you better color and a better viewing environment. Dell & Apple both make

good monitors (though there are others). Cheap is not good here though. Plan on $500 to $1,000 (though prices are dropping). Make sure you can do better than 1280 pixels wide for the resolution (1600 pixels wide or more is better for InDesign's control panel across the top of the working window).

Very large monitors

As you know, these are very expensive. A two monitor set up is often the best solution and supported out of the box by all Macs except the Mini. It usually requires a separate graphics card on a PC.

Storage: You need a fast, USB2 or better, external hard drive to back up your projects for storage. You also need a DVD burner to make off-site backups. Remember, a fire that wipes out your office also wipes out your external hard drive. Increasingly, there are online backup solutions to solve this problem.

Software: If you are buying, you need the Adobe Creative Suite Design Premium. We know it is $1,000 software. But non-profits can buy it from Adobe for well under $500, in most cases. Go to http://www.adobe.com/nonprofit and check it out. You need InDesign, Illustrator, Photoshop, and Acrobat Professional for professional production, at the least. You will also need Dreamweaver for Web production.

Printers

Now that you have a functional system let's talk about printers. Your choices are large, but not as large as you think. Most suppliers do not offer professional PostScript printing systems. To get what you need, you'll usually need to buy or lease from the manufacturer or a print supplier.

The need for PostScript: All professional printing is done with PostScript printers (with the exception of the PDF printing presses now on the market). There are many reasons for this: halftones, separations, knockouts, bleeds, marks, and much more cannot be done without this page description language. It is the only way to get predictable color that will be reproducible at your printing company. It is really not an optional choice. You must do this.

Genuine Adobe© PostScript© 3: This is the minimum standard at this time. The problem is that you need to look for this capability and you will not find it through most office sources. It is not considered a need for internal office work (which is one of the reasons internal office work looks less than professional to a printer/designer's eye). Companies building printers with genuine PostScript make a short list:

- ✦ **Xerox:** The best for prosumers, but several of the cheaper models do not include PostScript or use an emulation — so you need to be careful.
- ✦ **Ricoh:** They have a few good solutions
- ✦ **Minolta:** They have some good ones also
- ✦ **Canon:** They are one of the best choices for digital printing presses, but the consumer models use a clone of PostScript at best
- ✦ **H-P:** They use a clone of PostScript
- ✦ **Brother:** Nope

- ✛ **Lexmark:** Nope
- ✛ **And the list goes on:** for consumer printers genuine PostScript is very rare

You can google for reasons why, but genuine Adobe PostScript will solve many of your printing problems. As mentioned, it really is not optional. The new PDF printers are not yet commonly available.

Tabloid Extra & Tabloid:

Being able to use 11"x 17" paper is essential also. Tabloid extra lets you print ink to the edge of the sheet, but it requires a trimmer/cutter, and a cutter will cost you from $500 up to several thousand dollars. Tabloid printers enable you to do simple letter-sized booklets. Most of you do these a lot.

To go beyond this is beyond the scope of most of you.

Yes, it is possible to have a complete in-house printing department. But we're talking large company or corporation, megachurch, or national non-profit to have the volume of printing that would make this justifiable. If you have specific questions, just write us at info@radiqx.com for help or directions to resources.

Outside suppliers: You supply the finished artwork and often take the job to many suppliers

Let's go through the different technologies and talk about where you will be using them and why.

Offset lithography: This is your technology of choice when you have large quantities of printing to do: 2,000 or more copies of a letter-sized sheet. Offset excels at tens of thousands of copies, booklets, books, direct mail, and the like. This is what used to be considered the professional choice. That is no longer true, but for long runs, or projects that need folding, or embossing, or stamping, or die-cutting, or anything else that works the surface of the paper hard, offset is often the only solution. The major problems at this point are the lack of trained labor and environmental issues.

Important general rule

The first thing to do on a project is contact the printing supplier and get their special instructions. Every printing company or print supplier has special requirements for their equipment.

They will often have it available in a downloadable PDF. At the very least they will be happy to send you back the info in an email.

It is likely that there will be too much data to write down to do this with a phone call. You need the instructions written down in any case.

For spot color, litho presses are often the only real choice available. There is still a huge amount of spot color printing done. Digital CMYK is coming down so far in price that it is getting ready to take over from spot color. But spot is often the only option that makes sense from an economic, bottom line point of view.

Spot tends to be more elegant. It is almost a necessity for non-profit fund raising. Fancy, slick CMYK work is commonly seen by donors as wasting money and really lowers the giving to the charity involved. And for long runs, it is far cheaper than four-color process (CMYK).

Offset is also where you go to get any appreciable quantity of large items like posters. The most common large offset sheet fed press is probably 26x40 and there are many that are up to 72-inch or 96-inch wide.

The most common use for these large presses is large signatures. A 40-inch press can easily handle a 16-page signature of letter-sized pages or a 32-page sig of 6x9 pages. This makes them dominant in books, especially books with color. It's hard to beat a 120 copy per minute digital press for B&W legal documents, but 500-page 2-color spot or a CMYK book is almost always printed on one of these large offset presses.

Electrostatic printing: This is now the dominant technology, but it has real limitations. As mentioned, thick areas of toner crack off so embossing, folding, and the like have to be carefully planned to avoid toner. Also most digital presses are 11x17 and slow. A 40" offset press can print 10,000 or more 26x40 sheets per hour. A digital press has trouble going much faster than 7,000 letter-sized pages an hour in black & white or 2,000 an hour for CMYK. But the afore mentioned digital presses can output completely assembled booklets that only need to have a cover added.

Digital presses are the masters of much business work which runs in 50 to 1,000 sheet runs. Increasingly people are only printing what they need for a particular meeting or event and no longer dealing with the 2,000 copy minimums common with offset. Now that CMYK is approaching a dime for a letter-sized sheet, full-color digital printing is really coming into its own.

Variable data: One of the real advantages of the modern digital press is that it can image a completely different page for every copy coming out at 120 copies a minute (or 60-100 per minute for CMYK). Most of them have limitations like only one 8.5x11 side per four- or 8-page signature. The procedure is to make a precisely structured comma- or tab-delimited document with all the fields properly named and the variable data in proceeding rows of the spreadsheet.

Then you go to Window> Automation> Data Merge and the data record is opened in the Data Merge panel. The field names are then inserted into the document from the DM panel. The rules are many and strict. This will take close attention to the documentation and probably a bit of practice until you get this added to your skill set.

Screen printing: Here you need to work closely with your supplier. Find out what file formats they can use and the limitations of their process. For example, screen prints on clothing are often limited to very coarse linescreens (25-line to 50-line). To use this effectively you might well have to make a careful PDF out of InDesign and then rasterize it in Photoshop. In Photoshop you can convert the images to the linescreen values you need in bitmap mode. Traditional CMYK is often not available. Even if the screen printer can handle high resolution, they often use a special Photoshop plug-in to convert your image to multiple spot colors to make it printable within the limitation of the screen printing process.

Digital mimeographs: These exceedingly economical duplicators work largely like electrostatic digital presses with some things you need to understand. They are a specialized choice: low resolution; Spot color only; and coarse registration.

Why would you want to go through all of this? Because of the money you can save in printing costs. We've done many projects that were indistinguishable from offset in four color spot color for a nickle a sheet or so. In addition, you can purchase these presses very cheaply. The last one we purchased cost $13,000 complete: $6,000 for the press, $3,000 for the PostScript RIP, and $1,000 for each separate color head. These are a common solution for churches and non-profits, in general.

Inkjet: Here again, your design requirements will vary a lot with the printers used. Large format and grand format are commonly designed at half-size or less with a resolution of 200 dpi or so. It all depends on the vendor. In most cases you will need a rasterized JPEG because that is all they will accept. Work closely with the supplier and follow their specs.

For the new high-speed inkjet presses, it should be close to the design procedures of a digital press, but contact the supplier for special instructions. So far, most of them are low resolution (maybe only 400 dpi). But they are supposed to be very fast and very cheap. This may be the technology that eliminates the need for a digital mimeograph. However, the cost of the presses means that this is not likely.

Vinyl cutting: This varies widely also, but here are the basics. They need a vector image: PDF or EPS; spot color only. A sharp knife traces the paths to cut the vinyl. There will be limitations in minimum width of the images or rules. Delicate details will be very difficult to install and very easy to damage. Colors available will be those offered by the vinyl supplier they use. Often they only have a dozen colors or less.

Letterpress: Foil and embossing stamps are simple black and white images with no gray or tints allowed. The basic idea is to make a special spot color called letterpress or something obvious. Make your letterpress images, color them that special spot color, and set them to overprint. Die cuts use narrow rules. We draw the cut shapes. A 1/2 point works well in most cases. Scores and perforations are usually indicated with a dashed rule. They will be output as a separate negative that will be sent to the letterpress shop to make the die. The printing cost is about the same as one-color spot plus the die.

Flexography: This is a very specialized letterpress variant that uses cylinder presses and a flexible plate. The flexible plate tends to make circles into ovals and strange things like that. Also flexo commonly has trouble with tints, often needing a separate plate for each tint. This is not a problem. Your supplier will have software to handle everything, BUT you certainly need to work with them and give them art within their specs. This is the common solution for packaging—especially items like salsa or dip containers.

Gravure & Dryography: These are expensive top-end solutions. We have no direct experience here, but the quality of the suppliers ensures that they will guide you carefully through the process for exceptional results. They are used when you have very long runs (gravure), or when you require very high quality with very tiny detail. Dryography commonly works in the 300+ plus linescreen arena. We've seen samples that were done at 700 lines-per inch with amazing detail.

Let's go on to using InDesign

Chapter Two: Setting up your software

Do you feel like you are fighting InDesign for control?

Again, we are assuming that you know how to run InDesign. We are also assuming that your production is a continuous flow, importing copy, creating graphics as needed, importing them, and writing in explanations of the graphics created as needed.

This is the normal procedure for everyone. What we want to do here is show you how to get control of your interface. For one of InDesign's primary benefits (even in relation to the other apps of the Creative Suite) is its ability to be customized to fit you like a glove. It can become a tool you use as habitually as an martial artist reacts to attacks.

Yes, much of this is review for some of you—but there is a lot we can all learn about streamlining our workspaces

Probably the most common expression of frustration from our students and apprentices is that of not being able to work smoothly toward a design solution. They are frustrated by the stops, restarts, and constant redoes in typography, color, and layout. They seem to be trying to beat InDesign into submission–& that does not work well at all.

Does this roughly approximate your work flow?

You know the routine. You open a new document. You add the type. Then you start formatting it. This involves setting up paragraphs as you want them for the project, selecting the sample paragraph (or simply leaving your insertion point in place) and then making a new style that picks up your new formatting. You make a shortcut for the style, but you can never remember what you are using this time.

Styles: You make several, if not many, styles in this way for each project. But finding them to individually update for design corrections is a major waste of time. Often you just say, *"Forget it! Styles are simply not worth it"*

Color: You mix all your colors in the Color & Gradient panels so they are never available to use in any styles you need. You are constantly looking at other pages to remember what you did there. Consistency is a real effort for you, and your designs suffer because of it.

Subtle controls: You are always having to remember to turn off Hyphenation for headers and lists. Balance line lengths is also usually an afterthought. Your indents seem random and they are rarely tied together into that potent look that makes a design work so well. Your justification settings are just set at the factory defaults because it just takes too much time to correct them into what you really need for the different paragraph styles you need & use in each project.

Local formatting: You know that local formatting is a No-No, but you're not sure why. You do not have time for anything else. Character styles are rarely used because they never work in every instance. Styles in general are just too much hassle.

Do you realize the depth and power of the controls built into InDesign?

One of the most talked about but seldom implemented attributes of InDesign (& increasingly in the entire Creative Suite) is the ability it gives you to mold the application into a layout tool that fits your working styles, that you can use habitually. It can be set up to enable you to design fluently using the software as an extension of your creative impulses.

Does all of this sound helpful?

Then you need desperately need a set of designed defaults!

Taking the time to design your defaults is a real sign of maturity in graphic design

Application defaults: These are the changes you make with no document open. We are assuming that you already take care of setting your desired stroke weight, default font, default stroke & fill, and all the rest. We're assuming that you are taking the time to carefully build a set of page setups that actually meet your normal workflow needs. Also assumed is that set of documents used as templates. Just setting these few settings can make your life a lot easier.

But this is just the beginning:

What you really need is a set of styles that you can apply easily, with little effort, that can be modified quickly, giving you global control of your document as you massage the copy and graphics into a presentation that works for your clients. First, let's talk about shortcuts and workspaces.

Setting up a functional workspace

Many people think this is no longer needed, but that is certainly not true. While CS4 does ship with 8 default workspaces, it is very likely that you will not like any of them. If you are left-handed like me, it is certain you will not like any of them. What you see below is the Getting Started workspace that opened by factory default when you first installed InDesign. You are not using that any more, but let's take a look at some of the problems.

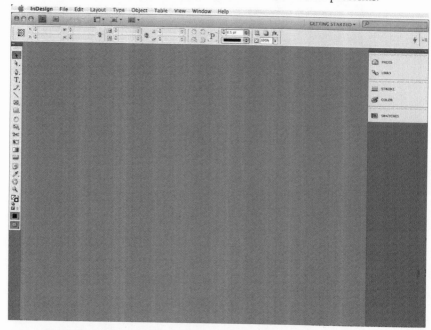

First the tools are on the left and the feeble panel choices are on the right. That may seem so normal to you that you do not consider how bad this setup is. *But consider this fact:* you find it easiest to reach toward the side of the monitor of your dominant hand. Many of you are right-handed, so the reach way across the screen for the tools is a real stretch for you. For lefties, the reach to the panels is just as long as Tools is for righties.

We have spent a lot of time researching the best setups for workspaces. What becomes immediately clear is that you need to do several things to make them work well and comfortably for you.

✛ **Tools:** This tool bar needs to be on your dominant side.

✛ **Most used panels:** these also need to be on your dominant side

✛ **Commonly used panels:** Should be on your non-dominant side

✛ **Rarely used panels:** can be left in their menu to be accessed only as necessary

Making these determinations

Obviously this takes a bit of thought. You have to decide which panels you use the most. In our case, they are the Paragraph styles, Swatches, and Effects. Place them at the center of the screen vertically, docked on your dominant side.

Most used: For the rest you have to simply practice. Watch yourself as you work and you will quickly discover which panels you use all the time. It is likely that this will be from six to a dozen or so. Again in our case, there are eleven. These are the panels we use several times an hour.

Commonly used: There are thirteen panels that we use daily or at least several times a week. We dock them in icons on our non-dominant side. We have a left-handed and a right-handed setup available on all our computers. For large operations, these two setups need to be standardized, of course. But consult carefully with your team to find out what works and take regular feedback to continually update these setups. The left-handed setup takes special care because all computers and keyboards are designed for right-handed users.

The InDesign team is convinced that you'll want several specialized setups. We do not find that to be true. Like tai chi, we have found that there is great value in repetition and habitual use. You can train your body to the point where you think "I need a drop shadow." Your eye and your hand arrive at the panel in the same instant.

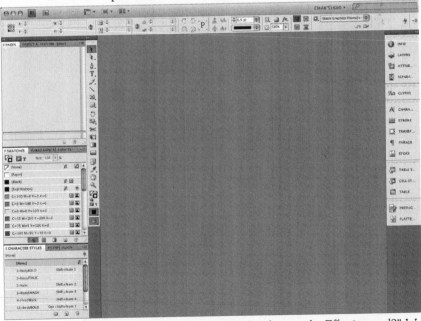

There is no conscious thought of "Where is the Effects panel?" We think of an effect needed and the body, eye, and brain go there and do it. Often the mouse is there before any of us consciously see the panel. The current lefty setup we use is above.

We have noticed though, that we do use different workspaces—to compensate for different monitors. For the tiny screen of a 13-inch MacBook all the panels are iconized—there is not room for expanded panels. Each setup takes into consideration the pixel width of the monitor.

Actually, the capture on the previous page is not accurate because we made it much smaller than actual size so you could see the names of the panels and how they are located. The actual 1600 pixel wide workspace looks more like this. You can see that there is a lot of space for the document. For the commonly used panels, there is room to leave the names of them partially open to help us remember what the icons mean on those panels used only every other week or so. As you can see there is plenty of room with a letter-sized page.

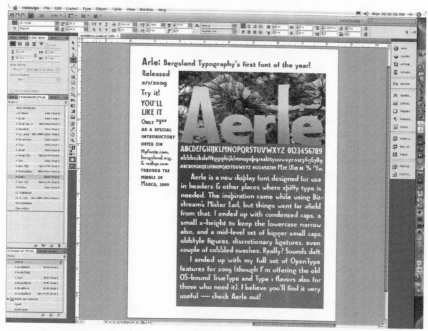

For CS5: We are still working out the new workspaces. It remains to be seen if we actually add the panels for all the new interactive and presentation capabilities. For book layouts, nothing has changed. But these workspaces are always an ongoing evolution.

Workspace foibles

The main complaint about workspaces is the inability to have more than one panel at a time open in each iconized dock. This is a minor issue simply solved by leaving all of your most used panels open on your dominant side like you see above.

Here's the list we are currently giving our apprentices. It is a basic set of panels that we believe you need to have open all the time. It's just a starting point. Let's give the list with a brief explanation of the reasoning for each.

Most used: Full width panels

As we just mentioned, one of the real frustrations with docked panels is that you can only have one open at a time. Also mentioned, our solution is to leave the most used panels open all the time at the same time. We leave them full width. The tab groups are chosen so we can always have three panels open at once. We've tried four tab groups, but that usually severely cramps the styles or swatches or pages visible at one time. So, at present, we are using these three tab groups. Obviously, you need to adjust this to fit your personal working style—as we have done.

The Top Tab Group

- **Object Styles:** Anchored objects are a pain to control without object styles

- **Text Wrap:** This one depends on your personal use

- **Links:** We use this constantly, even more than pages

- **Pages:** This depends on whether you do multi-page documents. Almost all of ours have at least two pages, usually several dozen, and often several hundred pages.

The Middle Tab Group (the most used panels)

- **Swatches:** We'll cover this later this chapter, but this is one of the real strengths of InDesign. It makes the Color and Gradient panels obsolete—along with the separate swatch libraries you're forced to use in Illustrator.

- **Paragraph styles:** Our most used panel after swatches

- **Effects:** Used several times a day or more

The Bottom Tab Group

- **Character Styles:** Used constantly for nested styles and the like. It needs to be in a separate group from Paragraph styles as it is often used at the same time.

- **Pathfinder:** This one is better than Illustrator's version because the choices are more limited and you do not have to expand all the operations. It also has Open & Close paths, plus a reverse path direction button for help with composite paths and fills.

Constantly evolving: We are constantly looking for ways to make our workspaces more useful, so they evolve over time. Yours should also.

Commonly used: In Icons (maybe with names showing)

These go on your non-dominant side, either iconized or barely open to see enough of the name to remember what those obscure little graphics mean. These are opened one at a time, plus you can set them up to auto-close in Preferences. It's nice to be able to keep them out of the way.

The tab groups: On this side these groupings are not nearly so important because you can only have one panel in the entire dock open at one time. Many people find this fact very irritating.

Tab group

+ **Layers:** We put this there because our apprentices think this is a good thing even though layers cause them more problems than they ever help. We use it very rarely.

+ **Attributes:** If you're working spot color, you'll need this a lot to set overprints.

+ **Info:** Questionable, but some use it a lot.

Tab group

The first three in this group are not often used, because most of these options are in the Control panel across the top. But when you want to format an entire text frame that is selected with the selection tool, this is the fastest way to do it (unless you simply format it by shortcut with a style).

+ **Character**

+ **Paragraph**

+ **Transform**

+ **Story:** Optical margin alignment. You need to add this to your repertoire if you're not using it already.

Tab group

+ **Glyphs:** We keep this in a separate tab group so we can have it open large enough to fill the screen. It is very important with Pro fonts that have hundreds of additional characters. Many of these special Characters are alternatives that do not show up automatically. The more you get into typographic control, readability and the beauty of excellent type, the more you will use this panel. It is the only way to access characters that do not have keyboard or OpenType feature access.

Tab group

+ **Stroke:** As mentioned, this ended up over here because it is always used and then immediately closed for some other panel. Your use may well be different.

- ⊕ **Align:** You can align or distribute any way you can imagine. It is an excellent panel. We don't use it much because most of our pages are a single unit with even the graphics anchored.

Tab group

Tables: the next three might go on the most used side, depending on how many tables you use. We use them regularly but not constantly, so we keep them over here.

- ⊕ **Table**
- ⊕ **Table styles**
- ⊕ **Cell styles**

Tab group

These are the panels used when you get ready for final output as you send your files to the printing company you are using.

- ⊕ **Separations Preview:** This is critical to make sure everything is separated properly and no extra colors have slipped in.
- ⊕ **Preflight**
- ⊕ **Flattener Preview**
- ⊕ **Trap Presets**

Tab group

- ⊕ **All the interactive stuff:** We have them here in CS5, but we never use them (so far). It sounds like something fun to play with, but we really have no use for these capabilities at present.

Save your workspace

We know this does not really need to be said, but we decided a subhead was needed and it is surprising how often we forget to save something very basic like this.

As you start this process, you'll be resaving your workspace under the same name many times a day. Once you get things comfortable, you'll not have to worry about it very often. The last time we had to make a major adjustment was today as I rewrote this piece. Before that it was when we got the little MacBook for presentations and that was over five years ago now (or was it six?).

Moving your workspace: Your workspace file is simply an XML document that you can easily install on any computer you use. Carry it (and your shortcuts) around on your jump drive. This is especially helpful if you are working in a department with many people and multiple shifts.

Where it's located

As you can see below, the path is User> Library> Preferences> Adobe InDesign> Version 6.0> Workspaces. Copy that to your portable drive and then you can simply drop it in the same place on any computer you are working on. Because it is XML, it should work pretty well across platform also.

Customized shortcuts

This is the next major point of timesaving efficiency. There are several (or many, depending on your use) shortcuts you really need to customize and add to your personal set. But first the basic arguments:

Throughout this book, we are going to do our best to scrupulously avoid listing default shortcuts. This is not because they are not crucial to efficient production. They certainly are essential. In fact, as one of our students accused one of us, several years ago, "After rejecting DOS because of its code and turning to a GUI, you are now advocating code again." As a retired programmer, in the industry since the 1950s, he found this to be nearly hysterical.

Keyboard shortcuts are a production necessity.

Let us state emphatically, keyboard shortcuts are not an option: They are a production necessity. With the production speed required by our industry, there is no way you can keep up without fluid use of keyboard shortcuts. However, shortcuts are a very personal thing. Any of us could offer our personal set of shortcuts, but they would probably help only a few of you. This is because we have each have analyzed our particular production style and methods – noting which tasks we use repetitively. We then learn the shortcuts that save us the most time. Most of you will have a great deal of trouble remembering more than a couple of hundred shortcuts, and it takes over 200 to run InDesign, Illustrator, or Photoshop alone. Thankfully Quark is but a memory—it took several hundred shortcuts to run it efficiently.

The good news is that all the apps in the suite now offer customized shortcuts. In general, if you find yourself using a shortcut and it is the wrong shortcut—don't relearn a new shortcut unless you have to. Simply change it

Setting the shortcuts

The keyboard shortcuts dialog box is found at the bottom of the Edit menu. It's a pretty obvious procedure. The dialog will force you to save a custom set as soon as you try to change one shortcut.

Remember the context: You can make shortcuts that only work in type, or in tables, and so on. You can use the same shortcut in several situation for different commands.

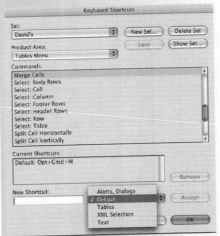

The path for the shortcuts XML file is the same as for workspaces: except that it is in the InDesign Shortcut Sets folder.

to the one you remember. InDesign is the best at this, because every command in the interface can be changed and you can use the same shortcut in different contexts.

Left-handed shortcuts

If you are left-handed (supposedly the majority of designers are — because we are right brained) your shortcuts will probably be very different than your right-handed colleagues. We will mention this heresy (to the normal world) because it is nearly normal in the design community (probably over half). All shortcut setups are right-handed. By this we mean that for those of us who use the mouse with one hand and execute the shortcuts with the other, lefties have a problem. (Many laptop keyboards are even more strongly right-handed with the elimination of the modifier keys on the right side of those tiny key collections.)

Think about all of the shortcuts built around A, S, D, C, Z, X, C, V. All of those keys are found at the lower left of the keyboard. Seemingly these would work well for lefties. However, in most cases,

they mean we have to drop the mouse. As a result, we have experienced large production speed increases by simply basing many of our shortcuts on the , . / \ [ ] l ; ' i o p keys in the right side instead. For example, in InDesign a sinister person (no bigotry there ;-) can access the selection tool with Command+', the direct selection tool with Command+\, and so on. This works, but it makes a lefty shortcut set much different than the norm. In fact, we can leave both right and left side shortcuts in place to be used interchangeably — depending on which hand is using the mouse at the time. Yes, most of us lefties are at least partially ambidextrous (by necessity in a right-handed world).

The point is simple, however. Now you are free to set them up the way that works best for you. More importantly, you can set them up in the way that you can remember. We all have limited memory, we need to streamline our shortcuts so we can produce as much as possible with keyboard shortcuts.

Timing concerns

We need to review basic production speed issues. The figures we are giving here are only approximate, but they are proportionally accurate.

✤ **Mousing menu commands:** 2-5 seconds or more—much more if you have go off into a hierarchical menu or two

✤ **Mousing panel clicks:** 1-2 seconds or more

✤ **Keyboard shortcut:** 2/10 of a second or less

To give a practical example, used many times a day: switching to the Selection or Direct Selection tool. If you are in text, you can type ESC. Then you can type the shortcut for the selection tool of your choice. But ESC only works if you are using the Type tool. (Obviously, it's much worse if you can't remember those shortcuts and have to mouse over to the tools and click on the tool of your choice.) It's an educated guess to say that you do this dozens, of not hundreds of times a day. If you make a custom short-cut that will force you out of any tool into the Selection tool of your choice you can save a minute for every 20 times or so (as mentioned for lefties try Command+' for Selection and Command+\ for Direct Selection). That's 2-5 minutes a day, nearly a half hour a week, and so on.

 Adding modifiers to tool shortcuts: InDesign is the only app to allow you to add the Command key (or any modifier) to the single letter shortcuts for the tools. Remember, you cannot use single letter shortcuts while writing in text—that letter is simply added to the copy. So even if you like the A & V [the normal shortcut for Select and Direct Select) you'll need a shortcut with a modifier key. It'll not only force you out of text frames, but out of any tool you are using.

Escape key: Yes, the Escape key forces you out of the text frame and into the last selection tool you used. But we regularly want the other tool—or another tool. The Command key shortcuts just mentioned save an amazing amount of time. You should try it. For right-handers, you might want to try the Command or Control key with a function key or a number as almost all the shortcuts on the left side of the keyboard are used up already. You will truly thank us if you get this set up for yourself.

The time savings mentioned so far may seem insignificant, but there is a real reason why we cantankerous ol'farts can beat you young whip-persnappers by hours. The going rate for formatting a book like this one is about 5 minutes per page. This includes importing the copy, formatting it, dropping in the graphics, eliminating widows and orphans, spell checking, and printing a proof. We bid it out with the expectation of producing an average of approximately twenty pages per hour. Without the shortcuts, it would be unfair to expect more than a half dozen pages or so.

The practical shortcut approach

You need to watch yourself work. This is why this diatribe is in an early chapter of this book. Notice which commands you use constantly. Learn the shortcuts for those commands. If you find yourself regularly using (or starting to use) a command from another application by mistake, change InDesign's to match your normal usage. Do whatever you are enabled to do to make your shortcuts common to as many programs as possible.

Obviously, this will take some time and effort. Of course, you will not be able to do this until you are in a daily creation and/or production environment. All of your competitors are doing it (especially those who can out produce you by a factor of two or three times).

The faster you can produce the more time there is to create.

A while back, one of our students was entering a major state of panic. He had been working on this twenty-four-page event program (that had to proof the next day) for about three weeks. He created (or subcontracted to other students) all of the ads (about thirty-five of them). He found someone to type all of the copy, set up a style palette, and format everything. But the project was just going so slow. His major concern was simply keeping track of all the pieces. (He had never done this before.)

Isn't this the bottom line?

We all got into this to enjoy creating, right? Isn't it strange that productive creation time is dependent on quick production techniques?

When he left class the afternoon before the deadline, he was basically a quivering mass of jelly laced with electrical charges (yes, he was nearly spastic). After he left, one of us took mercy on him, made two brand new documents (cover and insides), tossed everything into them, made master pages, dropped in all the ads, and roughly formatted everything in about 50 minutes. (He had told us what he wanted to do.)

Now, most of you probably have more experience than this man. He was a first-termer, working his first major project. However, we would guess that anyone at our experience level could do the same to you. *(If you are at our experience level, why are you reading this book?)* The time difference might not be quite as dramatic, but it would be substantial. This is the difference a computer set up to your specs, using your customized shortcuts, with applications of your choice, can make.

Remember, we are not talking right or wrong. The focus is on what works and what hinders production speed. Eliminate what hinders and focus on what works best for you. If you want to see our left-handed shortcuts for InDesign, go to http://www.radiqx.com/academy/training.html.

 One group for which you definitely need to define custom shortcuts are the four used to Change Case in copy: lowercase, all caps, title case, and sentence case. We have found that Command+Shift+9 & 10 & 11 & 12 work for most people. We set that up for a 65-person prepress operation and the time savings were phenomenal.

There's one more step before we can move on

A designed palette of swatches

One of the things that trips up most designers when they start using styles is the fact that styles can only use colors that are already set up as swatches. This may seem like another hassle, but in fact it is a blessing in disguise. This situation forces you to set up a designed set of swatches.

Why would you want a special color palette? That is obvious once you think about it. Your color choices are as much a core part of your personal style as the typography & layout choices. We all have a constantly evolving set of colors we use. For most of us (at least at the beginning) these color choices change with fashion. For many of us, these fashion choices remain a key part of our evolving design sense.

What is clear is the factory defaults are ugly

CMY & RGB are building blocks of color. They are not to be used alone except in those rare instances where magenta is actually a stylistic statement you want to make. It makes no difference if you like pastels or jewel tones; bold, saturated hues or subtle shades of color. The only universal constant is that no one except the laziest designers uses CMYRGorB.

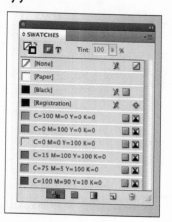

My experience is that we all need the six basic hues (red, orange, yellow, green, blue, & violet), some selected tints of those hues, plus a few gradients. All of these things are necessary for use in developing a gorgeous, truly useful set of styles. Remember, if you do not have them in Swatches, you are going to have to constantly save your style temporarily to go back and make any swatches you need. Then you have to edit the style again to add the colors you just made.

You will need a new color palette every 6 months, at least

In February, the Spring set needs to be implemented. In June, the Fall set becomes necessary. If you are like us, every July, you go to the best local department store to see the new fashion colors and make some decisions as to which of the colors presented are actually going to sell—become popular.

We find that trying to save these two palettes from year to year is not helpful because our sense of color is constantly evolving and we do not want last year's colors to corrupt our new palette. We serve clients where a sense of style and knowledge of fashion is critical—even if your style is timeless and classic.

Our current set

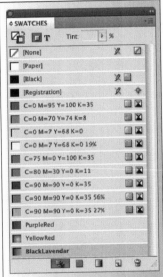

To the left you can see what we are currently using. It probably does not match what you like. But it is probably better than the defaults being currently used by you unless you've customized them.

Controlling the global look with different clients

Because all styles have this color palette embedded, when we change clients we merely have to modify the existing swatches to completely change the color styling of the piece. To replace a tint of the purple with one of the red, you simply make the new tint and then take the purple tint and delete it. This gives you the dialog that allows you to substitute the new tint for all the instances of the existing tint. You can see that option below.

In this way, you can easily modify the custom palette to bring it in line with the needs of your differing clients. You can also automate the application of these colors with the designed set of styles that we'll cover soon.

Important tip!

Every time you change the defaults, quit InDesign and reopen it to save your new defaults. The defaults are saved upon quitting the application. If you do not quit, you will lose your defaults if the app or the computer locks up or crashes before you can quit the app. Change defaults, quit, & relaunch InDesign every time and you will save yourself quite a bit of heartache.

Preparing to set defaults

We mentioned earlier that InDesign uses PageMaker's model that has both Application and Document Defaults. It is the best way to handle things. A copy of these defaults is saved automatically every time you quit InDesign (close the application). Application defaults control what happens every time you open a new document. Document defaults control what happens when you reopen an old document.

Application defaults: These are made by changing anything possible with no document open. This would include palette positions, palette contents, page size, margins, text frame options, style palettes for character, paragraph, objects, tables, and cells, swatches, stroke, almost anything in the application.

Document defaults: These allow you to do the same thing in a document you are currently working with. For example, there are fairly elaborate defaults set up for this book. Defaults like sections, master pages and so forth can only be done to a document. This is how templates (or resaving existing documents) help production speed so much.

This is all personal

As we go through this book we will continuously be suggesting application or document defaults you might find useful. However, all we can do is share our opinions. There is no right or wrong here either. This is why digital publishing and graphic design are so difficult. You have to understand all of the options and then set them up so they work for you.

Again, this is not a little thing. Your survival in the field is dependent upon functional defaults. Without them, your work speed will be so compromised (when compared to your competition) that adequate income will prove to be much more difficult to find (unless you work 16 hours a day – and you will probably have to do that regardless).

What kind of defaults are needed?

As much as possible, you need to have your application set up so upon opening a new document you can simply start working. Most of us have a standard document type that we use most commonly. For our operation, we have about 10 new document presets set up as you see to the left. We have a "normal" color palette that we use. Our text wrap is always set and so forth.

When we have another document to create, we can simply hit Command+N >>> choose preset >>> Enter, click in the automatic text box, hit Command+6 for the headline, and start typing. The styles are all set up to flow into one another. Once we start writing (or editing), creation becomes almost automated. All our tools are in the same place every day. We all have our personal workspace installed on all the computers, so when any of us on any of our computers reach for a tool or panel they are there.

However, standard defaults are not enough, even though they are essential. All of us have many "normal" documents. We meet that need by cataloging documents to be used as templates. These are documents saved with customized document defaults to enable them to be used as easily as your normal defaults for your most common documents. All that has to be done is import all text styles, import swatches, import object styles, and so on. We rarely even have to open these stored documents because we usually follow the procedure seen to the left.

The key thing to remember about these things is not how well organized we are — for we are certainly not. Think absent-minded professor and you have a closer idea. Think about how easy it must be to do these things if even Chak can get this together. ;-) Most importantly, having these templates allows us to keep track of the different organizational images. Plus, and this is key, the use of these templates probably saves each of us 150 to 200 hours per year or more (a good set of application defaults can save you a half hour to an hour for every new document you open).

Why spend all this time?

You don't have to, and as our competitor we hope you don't. As your friend we want to assure you that this will greatly enhance your ability to have fun as a designer. By setting up preferences and defaults, you can free up more time for design, and that is why we got into this career in the first place, right?

The important thing to remember is that setting up preferences and defaults is an occasional thing. If you don't take the time to do this, you have to do the same things for every document regardless. You may get very fast at set up, but it won't compete with someone like me who simply opens a template and starts work. Basically, we will start with a 15-minute to 1-hour lead in our production for every project. You really cannot afford this kind of competitive disadvantage.

The main thing that most designers miss is how comprehensive a good set of defaults can be.

Benefits of Styles

🔊 **Consistency:** Styles are really the only way to keep a long document consistent throughout the document, from issue to issue.

🔊 **Global control:** They are the effortless way to make changes to the overall look of an entire document.

🔊 **Production speed:** Once implemented they greatly increase production speed. Formatting copy becomes a breeze.

🔊 **Reduction of printing problems:** Good use of styles greatly reduces the number one cause of printing problems—extraneous fonts.

🔊 **Fluidity:** Page layout becomes a malleable art form flowing to fit.

🔊 **Reflow:** Documents that are a little too long or a little too short can be fixed by changing a style—as was done in this list.

🔊 **Instinctual formatting:** Styles will enable you to format copy habitually, without conscious thought. You think headline—and the paragraph is formatted to the headline style. Like in martial arts, you practice and practice until you react instinctively to an attack. With a good set of styles you can format without having to consciously think about how or where that style is.

🔊 **Preformatting:** A good set of styles will allow you to set up the look of a document before you add the first word of copy.

Styles impelled by your creativity

Default styles: One of the most needed, yet rarely implemented, default setups in the graphic designer's arsenal is a complete set of styles: paragraph, character, object, table, & cell. You need a functional set of default styles in all types that fit your workflow & your sense of style.

Styles that flow habitually

What is needed is a slight attitude adjustment. Imagine that you have a set of styles that you can apply habitually, *without conscious thought*, as you create any new project. Imagine how much time this would save. Imagine how much global control this will give you as you massage your copy into your page layout structures.

This is our goal here: to give you a sense that this type of workflow is not only to be highly desired, but that it is possible.

As usual, all we can do is share what we have learned and show you a suggested set of standard styles. We just want to give you a starting point that you can make your own. Again, as with keyboard shortcuts in general, the important thing is to design a standard set of styles palettes that will meet your needs without thought. To rephrase, it is possible to have a set of styles that apply to virtually all situations. All it takes is a little thought, creative inspiration, and some planning.

As mentioned a couple of times already, it will help if you think of this like Tai Chi training. Most of us have seen the classes in the park slowly going through the motions. But what is the goal of all of this—originally? It was to train your body in these movements until they become habitual. This is a martial art. The desired result is a set of movements that happen as automatic habitual responses to any situation.

To rephrase, it is possible to have a set of styles that apply to virtually all situations

If you think about the styles you use (or should use), it should be obvious that there are four styles which are used in virtually every project: body copy; hanging body for lists; headline; and subhead 1. In addition, it is helpful to add five more styles built off body copy plus four more built off headline (plus a few others that are personal to you for specific needs).

If you're working on a poster: your body copy will, of necessity, be a lot larger due to the reading conditions. Though you read books at the normal reading distance of about 18 inches, posters are originally seen from quite a distance and read from at least three feet away. Because the normal reading distance is at least twice as far, body copy needs to be at least twice as large.

The new concept is simple:
Format first — then modify the applied styles

All you need to do is rough format the copy as you enter it. You will find that it is easy to just make simple distinctions like body copy, list, head, & subhead. This can be done whether you are dealing with a business card, a flyer, or a large poster. Do not worry about what the things look like at this point. The new concept to grasp is that this roughly formatted copy can be massaged into form much more easily by modifying and adjusting styles that already exist and are already applied.

Paragraph Styles &
Character Styles panels

These two styles panels are the enabling concept for typographic fluidity and production speed. Styles panels are a collection of specialized typographic defaults that can be accessed at the click of a mouse or stroke of a key. You can set up styles for headlines, subheads, body copy, hanging indents, bylines, captions, tabular matter, or whatever your heart desires or imagines. Just keep your style list as simple as possible.

You can also set up very complex styles for graphic objects and most parts of a table. Basically, you can globally control the look of your entire document with a little practice — & believe us, you want to. We'll spend some time on Object Styles and anchored graphics later in the book. We'll also have a section on tables. But first let's learn the concepts on paragraphs like you see in front of you.

Let's start with
Paragraph Styles

These basic comments on paragraph styles mostly apply to the other different types of styles also. For most beginning designers, styles seem too complex to use—but believe us, they are not!

For most beginning designers, styles seem too complex to use; but believe us, they are not!

This frame is formatted by an object style that automatically formats the copy with two paragraph styles, and makes the round-cornered frame with specified insets to contain them.

It also makes this frame into an anchored object which can simply be pasted into the copy (in this case, in front of the "These two styles panels..." paragraph above), & it simply pops out here into the proper position automatically. It even has an automatic text wrap in case we decide to move it on top of some of the copy.

You get global control of the entire document if it is all formatted in styles: If you decide that you just don't like Baskerville for this project and want to use Caslon, simply change the relevant styles and the entire document changes. If you decide that your lists need 3 points before paragraph to help the spacing—*just change the style.*

Another problem solved elegantly by the use of paragraph styles is the situation where you end up with 16.5 pages of copy in a saddle-stitched booklet. The number of pages has to be divisible by four in saddle stitch binding, so you are forced to cut to 16 pages or stretch to 20. With a Style panel, you can simply cut the leading of the body copy paragraph style by a half point and save several inches (every 72 lines save half an inch if you cut the leading by only a half point).

There are many other global fixes like this that are an amazing help. You get global tracking control, consistent indents and alignments, nested character styles for an automatic progression of typographic styles within a paragraph or table, automatic paragraph rules and leaders for building forms and the like, automatic anchored graphics, automatic drop caps—plus much more at a speed that is phenomenal.

Based On *(Building Style Classifications)*

How many times do you design a simple flyer and change the fonts a dozen times or more? This is but one example of the time savings found in the global control of styles.

To make a good thing better, any style can be based on any other style. This means that when you change the first style, all the styles based on that style change also. The only things that do not change are the specific changes in the derivative styles. In most documents, all the headlines and subheads are tied together and all the body copy, hanging indents, bulleted lists, bylines, captions, and so on are tied together. In complex documents, there is often a third set of styles for the sidebar materials used to entertain the good readers.

If all the heads are based on Headline and all the copy is based on Body Copy, then an entire document can be reflowed by simply changing those two styles. If you do use the third sidebar set, you may have a third style to change — but this is barely a burden. This saves a lot of time—even on one- and two-page documents. You can imagine how much time it saves in books like this that can easily be three hundred pages or much more.

Next style *(auto-formatting your writing)*

To increase ease of use when writing (& InDesign is an excellent writing tool), any style can be set up to change to another when the Return/Enter key is struck. Again, this sounds like a little thing, but think about it. Every head, subhead, and specialized style in this book automatically returns to Body Text when the return is struck at the end of the header. This happens, on average, three times a page. It takes 3 seconds to pick up the mouse and click on the Style panel. This is the thirty-seventh page of the body copy and 50-100 heads so far. So I've saved 3-7 minutes so far with this simple setup. For 300 hundred pages, this next style option would save a total of maybe 2700 seconds, or forty-five minutes. That much saved time really builds up quickly. And this is but one simple example of savings. Once you begin using styles habitually you will find that you save many minutes or even hours per day.

In the sample to the right: all you have to do is set up the four styles before you begin. A **MEETING** style that changes to a **TOPIC** style that changes to a **SPEAKER** style that changes to a **LOCATION** style which has a **NEXT STYLE** back to **MEETING**. You will have to create the styles and then set the **NEXT STYLE** option. Once this is set up, you merely select the style for the first meeting and everything else formatted automatically: **MEETING** to **TOPIC** to **SPEAKER** to **LOCATION** to **MEETING** and so on. All you do is type and the returns cause the change to the new style.

Morning Inspiration: 8-9 am
TOPIC: GENUFLECTIONS

Minister of Procedure, Sir Hillary George
THE EAST VERANDA

General Session: 9-Noon
TOPIC: ANNUAL BUDGET

Chaired by Basil Rottenbothem
MAIN BALLROOM

Formal Luncheon: 1-3 pm
ENTERTAINMENT: THE ROLLING STONES

Bloviating by Hiz Oner, The Mayor
MAIN BALLROOM

Imagine how helpful this will be the next time you do a convention!

The white type in the paragraph rule, the size-length-color of the rule, the indents, the spaces before and after paragraphs, the font changes, the size changes, and all the rest were specified in the four styles. If you analyze the styles used in this book, you will see how much variety can be built into a style. You can genuinely make writing, or importing and formatting, a semiautomatic procedure.

As you can see, having a set of styles set up like this will save a great deal of time the next opportunity you have to set up a conference brochure. This entire booklet is formatted with the five styles panels. Much of the type styling is virtually automatic. All we have to do is remember the shortcuts when we have to start back with one of the heads. Of course, if we can't remember (or we have too many specialized styles) we can use Quick Apply – **COMMAND/CTRL+RETURN/ENTER**. Using a well set up styles panel, we can write and format as fast as we can type. Using the styles for everything we do means the shortcuts and style characteristics are firmly memorized and used habitually.

Copying (Loading Styles from other documents)

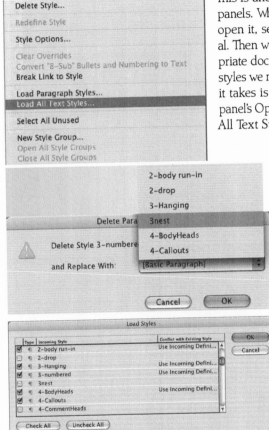

This is another powerful use of the style panels. When we start a new booklet, we open it, setting up the size, columns, et al. Then we load the styles from an appropriate document or template; and all the styles we need are dropped into place. All it takes is opening the Paragraph Styles panel's Options menu and using the Load All Text Styles... command.

With InDesign, we even get a choice of whether we use the formatting from the original and rename the existing style to avoid conflict or convert the formatting to the newly imported styles. Plus, we can get rid of a style by simply deleting the bad style and setting it to replace it with the style of our choice—and let InDesign reformat all affected paragraphs in the entire document automatically.

Because of their ability to reformat documents globally, Paragraph & Character Styles are indispensable. You should always use them unless you are setting only one or two lines of type.

Styles enable consistency. Once you make this into a habit, you will wonder how you ever managed without the control you get from styles.

Setting up a style — easily!

Capturing a style: The new Paragraph Style dialog box is complex. But once you understand that any paragraph setting can be captured, it gets easier. In most cases it is easier to set up a paragraph the way you want it. Then, with an insertion point in the paragraph choose the New Paragraph

Style... from the Option menu of Paragraph Styles panel or the Paragraph Control panel (or you can just click on the new style button at the bottom of the Paragraph Styles panel).

Let's go through the pages of the New Paragraph Style dialog box

Changes for CS4 As usual, the new version looks deceptively the same as CS3 and even CS2. The InDesign engineering team spends a great deal of time on small improvements. These improvements are often barely visible. However, the end result of all of them is a vastly improved workflow and greatly increased production speed.

General page

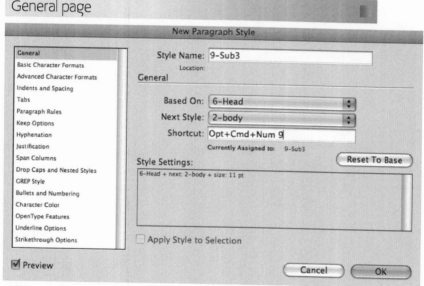

If you look at the page list in the column on the left side of the dialog box you will see that nothing has changed except for the addition of a Span Columns page. We will coer that biut of excitement in the book layout chapters

Style Name: We strongly suggest that you number all of yours using the number for used by your shortcut. It is a great aid to help you remember the shortcuts.

Based On: This will be the style you should have chosen before you opened the new style dialog box. Changing it retroactively does not always work well (but CS4 does it a lot better [click the Reset To Base button]). The new style is an exact copy of the style it is based on. Changes made in this new style will be the only commands NOT changed if you update the style it is based on.

For example, with the style of the previous paragraph, it is identical to the body copy style without a first line indent and with the addition of a nested character style and called 2-Body Run-In. 2-Body Run-In is used for the next paragraph also.

Next Style: As mentioned, you can use the next style setups to automatically format type as you type.

> **Yes, you must use the numerical keypad for style shortcuts. This is a real issue for laptops. You may need to buy an external keyboard or learn to use Quick Apply.**

Shortcut: Here we start getting to the production speed increases. On a PC we are very limited, but the 30+ shortcuts available still help a lot. You use any of the modifier keys (Control, Alt, and Shift) plus one of the numbers on the numerical keypad. The problem is that XP preempts many of these. Alt by itself cannot be used, plus several others simply are not available. We do not really know about Vista or Windows 7. We do not know anyone using them so far. But our PC friends are rare.

A Mac had nearly a hundred shortcuts available because it has four modifier keys through CS3: Command, Option, Control, and Shift. (CS4 has lost Control.) Even without the Control key there are 70 combinations or so. Almost all off these shortcuts can be used except for a few that are preempted by OSX (and you even have the option to turn off the OSX shortcuts if they interfere).

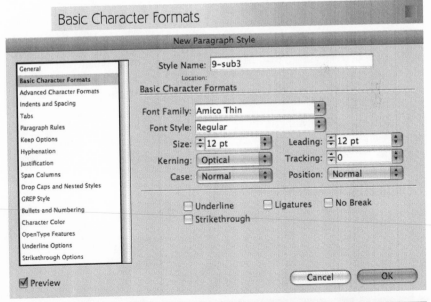

Basic Character Formats

As you can see, this page contains virtually everything in the Character panel. What isn't on this page is on the Advanced Character Formats page. You can control every aspect of font selection, size, leading, letterspacing, and scaling. The rest of the character formatting options have their own page. We'll discuss them as we go.

Very important!

Adjusting fields with Up & Down Arrow keys: We only mention this because it dumbfounds most of our apprentices (who usually come to us with only PC skills. Any field (Font Family, Font Style, Size, Leading, and so on) can be adjusted up or down by the use of the arrow keys. It is an amazing timesaver, as you can imagine. In fact, it saves so much time we have never even learned the shortcuts for larger and smaller. The arrow keys are easier to implement and faster as far as we can tell.

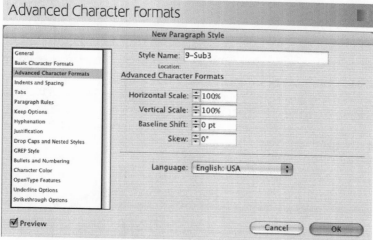

Here you see the rest of the Character panel. This is where you need to come for scaling, baseline shifts, and skew. This one is used a lot for bullets in a character style because many bullets need to be adjusted up and down with a baseline shift.

More importantly, this is where you pick the language used. As we get more and more into multi-lingual documents, this will become more important. We can easily see separate sets of styles for English, French, and Spanish (& more than that for EU stuff).

Indents & Spacing

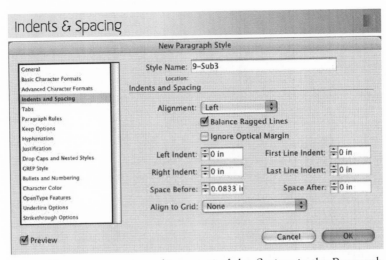

Here you can see we have most of the choices in the Paragraph panels except for the layout items like number of columns. The rest are on additional pages, like: Hyphenate, Drop Caps & Nested Styles, Bullets & Numbering, and most of the rest of the commands in the Paragraph panel Options menu.

This page is used very often. Much of the massaging of copy will be done by adjusting the space before and after paragraph. You will regularly be changing lists from Left to Left Justified and the reverse.

Again the arrow keys: remember, that the quickest way to adjust things is to tab to the field you want to change, then use the up and down arrows to adjust, then tab out to execute. If you need to readjust, Shift+Tab will take you back to do it again.

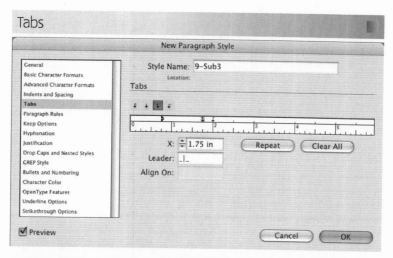

In this dialog is the complete Tabs panel: Each style can have its own set of tabs. This is where tabs really come into their own. You set tabs once per style and then apply them by style when you need them. As you will see when we get to the Forms section of this book, there are many virtually identical tabular settings needed for form design. Here is the tool you need to set forms by adding leaders throughout your document: much better than drawing rules and lining them up by hand.

The next four pages

Here we see the true use of these options: Here are the complete dialog boxes from the Paragraph Options Menu flyout: Paragraph Rules, Hyphenation, Keep Options, and Justification.

What you will discover as you learn to add the controls in these options is that this is really where much of the difference between amateur and pro lies. You can do an awful lot with these controls to make your type look good semi-automatically.

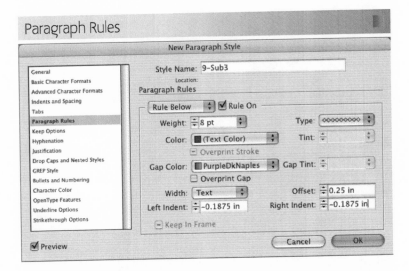

Paragraph rules are normally used only within paragraph styles: They are too tedious to use otherwise. However, once they are set up in a paragraph style the rules are added automatically every time you use that style.

TIP: If you understand how InDesign does rules, you see that each paragraph can have up to four rules attached to it: above paragraph, below paragraph, underline, and strikethrough. Any of these rules can use any of the stroke styles, be any color (including any color for any gaps in the stroke style), any width up to 1000 points, and any location up to 18 inches up or down. Paragraph rules can also be any length up to the width of the pasteboard so a rule in the narrow column can stretch across an entire page if that is what you need for your project. (Of course you can use more than this with rules applied by nested character styles.)

There is a great deal of room for experimentation

This means you can use a huge variety of rules to attract attention or divert it. You can make a rule that functions as an automatic tint box in back of your type. When you need them, they are available.

Basically rules (plus underlines & strikethroughs) are only limited by your imagination. They can certainly be overdone (we do that ourselves quite regularly by giving ourselves the *demo* excuse). But, they are excellent tools for directing the reader's eye — and for controlling emphasis.

Just be careful with type in a tint box: Doing this always reduces contrast and makes type harder to read. Be careful to compensate with font choices, point sizes, leading and the rest of the controls in our arsenal.

Keep Options

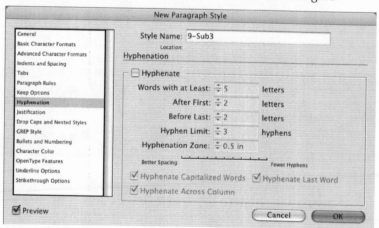

These options are used for almost every headline and subhead. Normally you want to fill in the field behind Keep With Next: with 2 or 3 lines. You certainly do not want a subhead or headline isolated by itself at the bottom of a column [this is the worst kind of paragraph orphan].

You also normally check the Keep Lines Together with All Lines in Paragraph for headers. For body copy we recommend Start: 2/End: 3. End: 2 lines often leaves you with a line and a partial line which does not look good.

This is also the place where you can set styles to start new articles or chapters and have them start on the next odd page (or even page or whatever you decide.) This all gives you an immense amount of automatic layout control.

Hyphenation

Again let's use headlines and subheads as an example. They should not hyphenate. In addition, often tightly written, terse lists with short paragraphs are set flush left with hyphenation turned off.

The actual hyphenation setup is something you want to determine before you even start putting together the documents. These settings are determined by grammarians and client usage.

Many say you cannot even have two hyphens in a row. Some say a hyphen every other row is terrible. Often you will have to make a case by case judgement as you massage the copy to fit your tidy, well-designed little boxes.

On the other hand, almost everyone agrees that agrees should not be hyphenated after the a in a-grees. Much of this is common sense. But be aware of the issue as some clients will have raging fits if you do not do it exactly the way they expected you to do it.

Justification

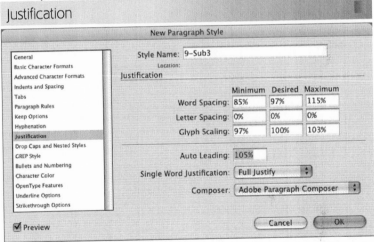

Normally these settings are only used when you make the setup for a newspaper or magazine. This is a place where the experts do not agree at all. Everyone has their own opinion. Our choice is to control the word spacing as tightly as possible to make a smooth type color. We go far beyond most recommendations.

In our experience, InDesign does justify exceptionally well. We have changed the default settings for Radiqx to 85% Min, 97% Desired, & 115% Max with superior results. Most say that Desired should always be 100%, but some fonts simply have space characters that are too wide. But these settings are part of your personal style.

However, you will want to regularly make Auto leading changes. It is true that auto-leading for body copy in almost always 120% (or 10/12). On the other hand, headers are commonly 105% for C&lc and 80% or less for all caps and small caps (that have no descender). Gradually, you will find that careful adjustments to a style here save you a lot of grief as you actually begin to flow copy into your document.

Span Columns **New for CS5**

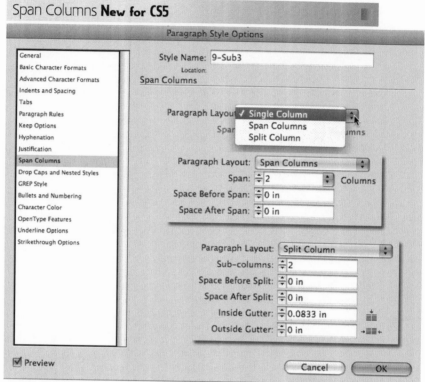

The three options are composited in the single image above. This has been the most demanded feature for InDesign for about three versions now. They got what they asked for, but...

Before you get too excited, this most demanded feature only works with columned text frames. It will not span a headline across threaded frames. When you think about that it immediately becomes obvious why this is so. However, text frames with multiple columns are really tedious to work with. In fact, they are so bad, we never use them.

What I am not sure of is if it will be faster and more efficient than the current necessity of placing headers like this in a separate text frame. However, we will cover the options in the book layout chapter toward the end of this book.

Split columns: On the other hand, split columns is very handy and you will probably use it a lot. We cover this on pages 62-63.

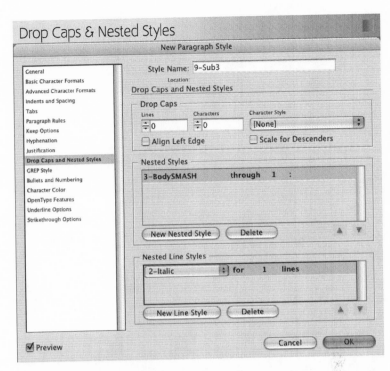

You can set a Character Style to use with your drop caps. That is commonly done because drop caps are often in a different font (at least). Drop caps in InDesign are much more powerful than many designers realize.

 Dropped In-Line Graphics: For example, as you can see to the left in this paragraph, we commonly place [import] a graphic at the beginning of a paragraph and then use the drop caps feature to lower the graphic 3 lines with the rest of the paragraph in a run-around. One time for a tall, narrow poster, we dropped the inline graphic 28 lines—down through seven or eight paragraphs below the insertion point.

Nested styles

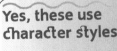

Yes, these use character styles

We will cover them next

We always used to call these run-in heads. Adobe's name indicates what they really are – because they are much more powerful than simple run-in heads. Simply put, a nested style allows you to automatically apply a character style to the start of the paragraph until a specified delimiter appears. You can have a bold style run-in until the first colon, for example. This is a very common addition to this book

Bold through colon: You've seen this through out the booklet. But we can easily add a second nested style through the first em-dash.

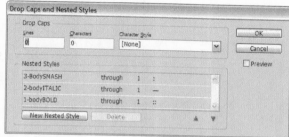

Italic through the em-dash – then back to normal copy. We could even add bold through a second colon – if we wanted [as you see below].

This is the set up we used for the next two paragraphs below. Notice we put two colons for the third run-in (it counts the first one used also). Once the style is set up we do not have to do a thing except type the copy or apply the shortcut to existing copy. The nested styles just appear like magic depending on your set up.

by David Bergsland – **Practical training in page layout:** *2000 On Word Press.* What an embarrassing book that first book was (though it's out of print)! This one seems a little better. We've learned a bit since then.

by God's inspiration – **Practical training in living:** now this is truly an excellent book!

Adding new character styles from within the new style dialog: Believe it or not, this is one of the major additions CS4 has added. In CS3 or earlier, we were constantly having to close out a partially finished style to add a character style for a drop cap, nested style, and so on [like we still must do with Swatches]. Now there is a New Character style choice in the popup menu. See character styles in chapter four.

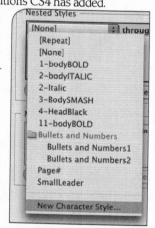

Nested Line styles: To be honest, we haven't played much with this one. It became available in CS4, but so far in two+ years, we've never found a use. But it would seem to be a nice addition to the repertoire. It allows you to be able to apply a Character Style by line. This has never been a style any of us liked. One of the more common uses is small caps for the first line.

The following was the fashion several years ago. The 1st line is in 18 point, the 2nd line in 16 point, the 3rd line in 14 point, and so on. We've also seen the 1st line Black, the 2nd line Bold, the 3rd line Demi, the 4th line Regular, the 5th line Light. You can do the same thing with colors—or with colors in addition to all these things.

To us, it's always seemed pretty desperate—a lack of a better idea. It draws too much attention to the type. However, typography should be invisible, simply displaying the content. *Remember!*

Typography should invisibly present the copy as almost irresistibly readable.

Bulleted & Numbered Lists

InDesign has finally reached the promise of earlier versions with its list options. At least it seems that way to us. Some still complain, but that's always the case. Part of it is being able to add new character styles on the run (see above). But in general, it now does what we expect when we choose an option. Maybe we've just been trained by the earlier versions.

Bulleted lists

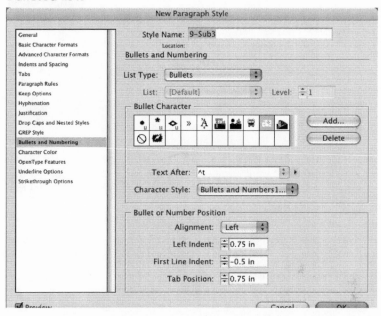

The bullets can be added from any font you have installed on your computer. You can use Unicode to specify a certain character that is available in any font (like a bullet) or a specific character from a specific font (like a dingbat). You can also format the bullets with a character style (a newly added one if that is necessary).

As mentioned earlier, the only real problem seems to be a necessity to add baseline shifts for dingbats in unusual fonts set at a larger or smaller size than the rest of the copy in the paragraph that follows the bullet.

Numbered lists

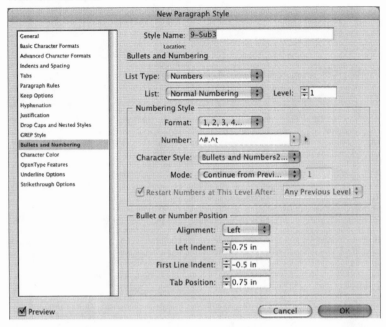

The numbered list options are more extensive yet. You have any of the numbering formats available to page numbering plus 01, 02 03, etc. You can specify how you want numbers and special characters added at the beginning of a paragraph with very few limitations. [You can't put a tab before the number, for example.]

You can apply a character style to the number to make it a different font, size, color, and so on. And finally under mode you have the choice of continuing from previous number or restarting at a specific number.

 Fixing numbering issues in the copy: If you choose Continue From Previous Number, you will regularly want to start over. With an insertion point in the paragraph, a simple right-click will give you the command to Restart Numbering.

Character color

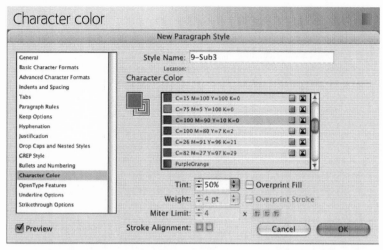

The key here is to remember that you can only choose from colors that have been added to the Swatches panel. That is why we covered that so intensively last chapter. You can file a feature request with Adobe to make an add new swatch option available like they did for the character styles in CS4. The address for that request on that Adobe site is currently:

http://www.adobe.com/cfusion/mmform/ index.cfm?name=wishform

You can pick a fill and stroke for each style. You can apply any color, tint or gradient that is in the Swatches panel (plus make tints of the solid colors). You can set Overprint options.

OpenType Features

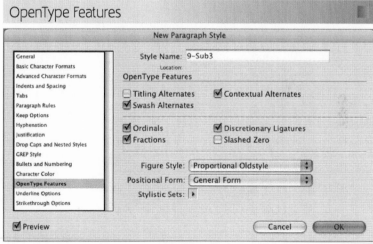

Here you can add Discretionary Ligatures, Fractions, Swashes, Titling Caps, Ordinals, and many of the other advanced typographic benefits of an OpenType Pro font.

Mainly this feature is used to pick the type of numbering you want to use. You should use lining figures for copy set in all caps or for accounting copy, oldstyle figures for lowercase copy, and small cap figures for copy set in small caps. (Small cap figures are very rare, however, so you may be forced to make a bad choice of lining or oldstyle with small caps.)

As you may have noticed, we have had the ordinals and discretionary ligatures turned on for the entire book. That may bother some of you. We feel that it enlivens the copy a skosh without affecting the color—makes it spiffy. Of course, David is going nuts and adding more ligatures with every new font release.

Underlines & Strikethroughs

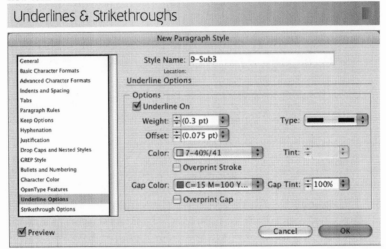

These options have all the power of paragraph rules but they apply to the specific words. In other words, you can use these options to add rules that appear on every line of a paragraph (unlike paragraph rules that can only appear once per paragraph).

As you can see to the left, this is the underline page. The options are the same for strikethroughs. They aren't used often, but they are an excellent way to add highlighting, for example, if you have a full color book.

Just remember to keep your set of styles as simple as possible!

Building A Set Of Character Styles

New Character Style

General	Style Name:	Character Style 1
Basic Character Formats	Location:	
Advanced Character Formats	Basic Character Formats	
Character Color		
OpenType Features	Font Family:	
Underline Options		
Strikethrough Options	Font Style:	Italic

Size: Leading:

Kerning: Tracking:

Case: Position:

☐ Underline   ☐ Ligatures   ☐ No Break
☐ Strikethrough

☐ Preview   (Cancel) (OK)

As you may have noticed, and will certainly see as we move on through this brief overview of Styles, is that character styles are a crucial part of Paragraph, Object, Table, and Cell styles. They give us the ability to format a portion of type within a paragraph. They are the solution to many problems you don't even know you have yet. The nested styles we have already covered are only one instance.

As you can see above, The New Character Styles box has many of the options of the New Paragraph Styles box. The options do not change, but all fields are left blank except the specific changes you want to make. You can see that the only change on this page is a style of Italic. *As you can see here where the style is applied,* the style alters nothing else in the paragraph.

Local formatting

 Local formatting is the major problem to professional production: One of the biggest temptations to new designers is to attempt to fix small problems, or create specialized paragraphs, by going directly to the Character or Paragraph panels and the formatting options found there. This is called **local formatting** because it only affects the paragraph(s) (or the words or letters) selected at the time.

There is a time and place for this. Local formatting is appropriate for eliminating widows and orphans and for adjusting vertical justification. The problem is that locally formatted type is not reformatted when the Styles panels are adjusted. In other words, local formatting removes the selection from the global control of the styles. This can be a real problem if you have a large document and can't remember any local formatting until you find the error after it is printed.

So, the rule is this:

Use local formatting only for final cleanup.

All local formatting should be done last, if possible. Its appropriate function is massaging the copy into its final configuration. Even then it should be done very sparingly. Extensive local adjustments can make simple reflow a nightmare costing an amazing amount of extra time and aggravation. That might not mean much to you now. But imagine making changes to a book like this if there were a lot of local formatting. It would take me many unplanned hours. We have just completely reformatted the book up to this point. We made many changes to styles and added (and subtracted) a lot of the original copy. So far, it has taken us about 10 hours to rewrite the first 50 pages. There are not more than a half dozen paragraphs so far that have any local formatting.

Let's rephrase the concept

The solution to local formatting—Character Styles: This panel enables you to format selected text. It is meant as an addition to the other Styles panels. One of the main reasons it is so nice is that you can change only what needs to be changed.

For example, I have a Bold style (I use Option 1 for the shortcut [Shift+1 on the PC because the Alt key is not available]) that does nothing but change selected words from whatever they were to **Amico Bold**. It does not change the point size, leading, or anything else, just the font and its style. I have an Italic style *that just changes the font to Italic, nothing else.*

The main thing enabled by the Character Styles panel is global control of local formatting. If you edit the Character style, everything formatted with that style is changed also. We am using nine character styles for this booklet (plus three more for Bullets & Numbering). We have found we always use three basic character styles – when we need to temporarily go to a different font, type color, or point size for some purpose. By doing all of our local formatting with the Character Styles we retain global control over the formatting with fluid layout.

Before character styles, all local formatting resulted in removing the type that was custom formatted from style panel control. Then, if a global change was made to any individual style, we would need to go back and find every locally formatted piece to change it to the new settings. Now all we have to do is change the Paragraph Styles and then change the Character Styles. In fact, it has gotten to the place where any local formatting usually means we just add another style: paragraph or character. That way we retain the global control needed for global formatting fluidity.

Another place that character styles are used
is for the table of contents

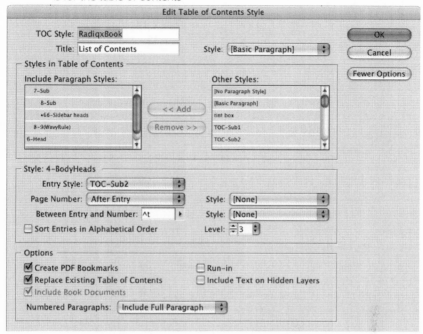

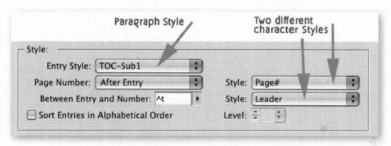

Tables of Contents are made by collecting the paragraph styles of your choice and adding page numbers if you desire. As you can see to the left, there is a lot of power available here.

For each paragraph style added to the TOC in the setup dialog box (found under the Layout menu), a separate TOC paragraph style should be made and each needs two character styles for the leader (or other spacing characters) and the page number. This means that you can have the leaders and page numbers look the same for all styles in your table of contents.

A basic set
of default styles

Before we get specific, let's review what the expected result will be. To give a personal example, we started using the shortcut Command+Num6 for headlines in PageMaker 4.2 almost 20 years ago. We developed a small, but complete, set of standard styles by 1993. We've been using these or a modification of these styles ever since. At this point, when we think we need a headline, our fingers automatically type the shortcut and the copy is formatted in the headline style. When we hit the return, it automatically changes to the body copy style, & so on.

We no longer have to remember the styles we use or the shortcuts for them. All we do is think that we need the second level of subhead and our fingers just type Command+Num8 and the formatting is applied to the copy we are working on.

Formatting becomes extremely fast, and automated. We can simply format focusing on the type of style needed and our fingers habitually apply the styles as needed. Conscious thought is not needed to format the paragraphs or to add most of the character styles.

Our current basic set of styles

At the bottom of the next page we will give you the standard set we teach our apprentices and on the top the set we use as the default here at Radiqx. The naming/numbering conventions you use is up to you, but the concept is important. Notice that many of our style names are abbreviated. In truth, by now we could simply use numbers for the names (they have become that automatic for us in our daily use).

When you use a standard palette like this, looking for these styles is simple — because they are always in the same place. For the longer documents (like our books, for example) you will probably need a full set to add sidebar styles and so forth. In fact, at this point, this book is using 38 paragraph styles so far. In a book that teaches the use of styles—some of which are very unusual—we could easily be at fifty styles or more before it is all written. Normally a basic default set of a dozen or so is sufficient. Take a look at the basic styles we start with next.

 Keeping styles in order: One of the irritating aspects of the most recent versions of InDesign is that the alphabetical order of the styles is not maintained. New styles are dropped below whatever style you have selected. The only solution is to select the **Sort by Name** command from the panel menu at the top right of the styles panel.

Of course, the actual styles used varies by job, but this is the default set of styles found in our Paragraph Styles panel for every new document:

⊕	[Basic Paragraph]	none
⊕	0 Kicker	Command+Num0
⊕	1 Dropped Graphics	Command+Num1
⊕	2 Body copy	Command+Num2
⊕	2 Body Run-in	Command+Option+Num2
⊕	2 No First	Command+Option+Shift+Num2
⊕	3 Hang Numbers	Command+Num3
⊕	3 Bullets	Command+Option+Num3
⊕	4 Body Heads	Command+Num4
⊕	4 Wavy Callout	Command+Option+4
⊕	5 Quote	Command+Num5
⊕	6 Headline	Command+Num6
⊕	7 Subhead 1	Command+Num7
⊕	8 Subhead 2	Command+Num8
⊕	8-9 Wavy Rule	Command+Option+Num8
⊕	9 Callout	Command+Num9

An abbreviated suggested set for you

You will need a place to start your setup. We have developed a starter set that will work fine for this. The instructions are found at:

http://www.radiqx.com/academy/default_styles.html

⊕	[Basic Paragraph]	none
⊕	0 Kicker	Command+Num0
⊕	1 Inline Dropped	Command+Num1
⊕	2 Body copy	Command+Num2
⊕	2 Body Run-in	Command+Option+Num2
⊕	2 No first	Command+Option+Shift+Num2
⊕	3 Bullets	Command+Num3
⊕	3 Numbers	Command+Option+Num3
⊕	4 Body Heads	Command+Num4
⊕	5 Quote	Command+Num5
⊕	6 Headline	Command+Num6
⊕	7 Subhead 1	Command+Num7
⊕	8 Subhead 2	Command+Num8
⊕	9 Callout	Command+Num9

The important thing to remember, when setting up your styles, is naming consistency. In our case, for example, Command+Num6 always gets us Headline; Command+Num3 always gets us some type of list; Command+Num7 always produces a second level subhead; and Command+Num9 always supplies a pull quote no matter what document we am working on. The key to quickly flowing production is simple — habitual formatting. We think headline and our hands hit Command+Num6 (without conscious thought).

 On a PC: When we are working on a Dell box with XP Pro, we have a lot of trouble implementing this strategy. There are simply not enough shortcuts available in Windows. The Alt key is almost completely co-opted by the operating system so it is not available. So we use another automated method: Quick apply.

Quick Apply: We have not found this to be really useful on a Mac because we usually have enough shortcuts and they are faster. But on a PC,

or any laptop with a limited key-board it may well be the only way to organize things. Remember, Ctrl+Enter (Command+Return) opens a list of the styles being used. Then just start typing the first letters of the style. When you get close use the arrow keys to go up or down until you have the style you want selected and then hit the return key to apply the style.

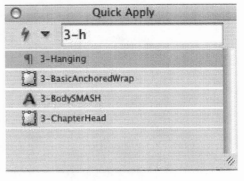

Styling tips for the basic set

Hopefully it is obvious in the lists of styles on page 57 that styles 1 through 5, and 9 are based upon 2 Body copy. Styles 7, 8, and 0 are all based on 6 Headline. We can change the fonts for the entire document by simply changing 2 Body and 6 Headline — talk about global document control! Even for small one-page documents habitual formatting can save you many minutes or more as you test fonts to determine what will work best for a particular client and project.

Please do not try to tell us that these tips are not necessary: In fact, they are becoming increasingly necessary to teach. In the new millennium we are dealing with designers who hate to read even though all they design are reading materials. Plus many designers are entirely self-taught. Everyone has a computer these days and anyone can buy the software. However, we can no longer assume they have read enough to recognize good typography and they almost never have any idea of the practicalities of paragraph design & page layout. The likelihood is that some of you are in this category so you have no idea what the norms are.

What we want to do here is give you some design tips to use when setting up your set of standard styles. We will go through the basic paragraph needs – explaining the hows and whys as we go. Again, some of our solutions will be different from some of yours. In most cases, we are just talking about normal usage. **You must come up with your own styles.** This is the core of your layout style. If you do not work on this, you'll pay for that lapse with the extra time spent – *non-billable and unpaid.* Plus, your typography will be haphazard & ineffective.

Dealing with the readable text

Major alignment changes:

New: One of the major typographic changes brought about by the new capabilities of InDesign's paragraph-level justification is the change from needing flush left for excellent body copy. Now, it is really true that: Excellent type color is produced better by justified copy *(assuming, of course, that you have column widths under control).*

The first assumption is that you have column widths in good, readable range. The formula we use for column width is very simple and shown in the sidebar on the next page.

2 Body copy

We should be able to assume you have this under control. These are the normal paragraphs of copy. The norm is 10/12 flush left or justified left. All the other alignment options are much more difficult to read. With a poster, flyer, or advertisement, you may well use centered or justified center. But if you do, be careful to break for sense. In other words, make each line break (soft return) fall between phrases or concepts to enable easy readability.

✤ **Size:** The standard for body copy is 10/12 with the point size varying from 9 to 12 point. The leading will be determined by the amount of line spacing built into the font used and the x-height. The norm is autoleading set at 120%. The larger the x-height, the more leading is needed. A small x-height, like this, may require a larger point size and less leading. Many publishers demand 10/12 no matter what—limiting font choices.

✤ **Invitations and the like:** When using script fonts 18/24 is the norm because of their severe legibility issues. In general, formality means increased white space. Scripts help this look with their extremely small x-heights and unusual letter shapes. But you need to get the x-height up to legible levels by using the larger point sizes.

- **For posters and flyers:** Body copy sizing needs to be multiplied by the reading distance. The norm of 10/12 is for normal reading distances of around 18 inches or 45 centimeters. If you expect the readers to be reading from 3 feet or a meter away, you will need to double the point size, at least. If they will be reading it at 180 inches (15 feet) or 4.5 meters, enlarge body copy point size by ten times or a little more.

- **Increased leading:** Longer line lengths or heavily stylized fonts require increased leading. This enables the reader to more easily find the beginning of the next line of type. If you use the 40% of the point size rule seen to the right, good readers should be able to scan straight down the column without moving their eyes from side to side. Formality also needs extra leading — plus a lighter, more elegant typestyle.

- **Paragraph spacing:**
Historically, with typewriters and word processors, you used either a first line indent or extra paragraph spacing, not both. For many of us now (though it is seen as heresy to the rigid), it is normal to see a first line indent with a couple of points of space before paragraph. You need to be careful though. If your design style requires that lines of type line up horizontally from column to column, you will not want to add space before or after your body copy paragraphs. You never have the same number of paragraphs per column so they will not line up.

Column width: a practical rule of thumb that's less complex than most:

40% of the body copy point size in inches: So, 10 point type works well in a column that is four inches wide (± 10%).

Note: This assumes a normal x-height of about 50% of the cap height. If the x-height or set width is radically different than the norm you will need to make adjustments.

- **First line indents:** There is no right or wrong about first line indents. The norm would be somewhere between 12 points to a half inch. Less than a quarter inch or 7 mm usually looks like a mistake. For highly stylized copy we have seen first line indents of half the column width with the first letter of the paragraph bumped up to two or three times the normal point size in a Raised Cap style. Readability is your guide, as always. The visual look needs to take second place. It may be important, but if the reader does not read it, you've wasted your budget.

Readability is your guide, as always.
If the readers don't read it,
you might as well burn the money spent.

3 Hanging body

Here the norm would be to make the left indent the same as the first line indent of 2 Body copy. The negative first line indent should be between half the left indent and all of it. In other words, the bullet should hang somewhere between the left column margin and the left indent.

✤ **Hand-setting numbered lists:** In earlier versions of InDesign, it was commonly necessary to add an additional tab and not use the automated lists. With a negative first line indent that is identical to the left indent of the style, you can then add a flush right tab an eighth inch to the left of the left indent. Doing this makes for better number alignment when you go from 9 to 10 or 99 to 100, for example. Of course, the Bullets and Numbering... dialog covers this fairly well in CS3 & CS4. However, there may still be times when you will have to set up tabs and enter the numbers by hand between the tabs.

✤ **Breaking for sense:** Watch your lists carefully.
Often these paragraphs are so short
that you have to break for sense
to get rid of the large amount of widows generated.
Extra care needs to be taken for readability.

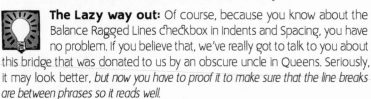

The Lazy way out: Of course, because you know about the Balance Ragged Lines checkbox in Indents and Spacing, you have no problem. If you believe that, we've really got to talk to you about this bridge that was donated to us by an obscure uncle in Queens. Seriously, it may look better, *but now you have to proof it to make sure that the line breaks are between phrases so it reads well.*

- ⊕ **Readability:** If your bulleted and numbered lists are crucial to reader understanding, you may want to make them larger, bolder, and/or in a different font than your body copy. They are very important. Make sure your readers notice them. However, if you overdo it, they just look gaudy (as they probably do in these examples).

Tab tips

Alignments, indents, and tabs are measured in relation to the column sides: except for the first-line indent. However, if you have curved frame edges the alignments & indents are in relation to the frame edge & the tabs are in relation to the bounding box. This means that curved left frame edges (or edges changed by text wraps), you need to hand space the tabs with fixed spaces: em, en, thin, & hair spaces.

- ⊕ **For tabs to work as you expect:** the alignment almost always needs to be flush left.

- ⊕ **All tabs and indents are tied to a paragraph:** You'll need a soft return to use them again in the same paragraph (of course, you can always use a paragraph style to hold your tab settings).

- ⊕ **You need to use a table for wrapping copy like descriptions:** Just set the borders to none.

New to CS5: Split columns

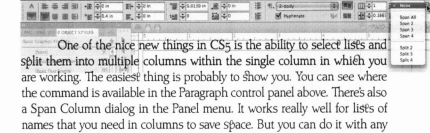

One of the nice new things in CS5 is the ability to select lists and split them into multiple columns within the single column in which you are working. The easiest thing is probably to show you. You can see where the command is available in the Paragraph control panel above. There's also a Span Column dialog in the Panel menu. It works really well for lists of names that you need in columns to save space. But you can do it with any selection of type.

Same paragraph split 2: One of the nice new things in CS5 is the ability to select paragraphs and/or lists and split them into multiple columns within the single column in which you are working. The easiest thing is probably to show you. You can see where the command is available in the Paragraph control panel above. There's also a Span Column dialog in the Panel menu. It works really well for lists of names that you need in columns to save space. But you can do it with any selection of type. Though you have to be careful widths get so narrow (like they are about readability when the column in this example).

Like I said, it is probably best used for lists of stuff:

✠ **Books**	✠ **Trains**	✠ **Fighters**
✠ **Boats**	✠ **Bikes**	✠ **Bombers**
✠ **Planes**	✠ **Planes**	✠ **Limos**

I just typed the list above. Selected it all and chose Split 3 from the drop-down menu in the control panel. This is a very nice feature.

Miscellaneous styles based on 2-body

✠ **Quotes:** These are usually indented left and right to the same amount as the first line indent, but this is certainly not written in stone. Quotes are also usually set justified when the body copy is flush left and often set flush left or centered when the body copy is justified. The main thing is to make them different enough so the quote is obviously a quote.

✠ **Bylines:** The name of the author of the article is set in many and various ways. Most common is same font as the body copy, flush right, often italic.

The author bio: You may also want to have an entirely different paragraph style at the end of the article with an indent that allows room for a small picture (add the pic as a drop cap to make it easy to format) and a short bio to go with the name and credits. The little bio can add a gentle warm fuzzy to help leave the reader with a good memory about the article. The bio is often set with the sidebar group of styles for impact (to make the author happy).

✠ **Captions:** This little item has changed greatly in the years we have set type. When we grew up, captions were commonly set small and italic. Current research suggests that the caption is commonly much more important than the headline in attracting readers. Current thought makes captions a little larger than body copy, flush left, with a synopsis of the points the article is making about the picture. In other words, because the picture is illustrating the article (why is it there if it is not?), the synopsis helps the reader decide whether or not to read the articles. Remember, if it is not important and/or make sense to the reader, he or she will be angry if you trick them into reading an article that has no relevance to their life.

New for CS5—automatic captions: This one passes me by, because as you have probably noticed I almost never use captions. I place the images within context so I don't think they are needed. But this is a very rare attitude and almost never seen. The basic idea revolves around large scale image management where the caption is written into one of the fields of the metadata for that image. Then you can simply right-click on the image and choose Captions > Captions setup to chose what pieces of metadata you wish to add and where you want to add it.

Issues: When you then right-click on the image and choose Captions > Generate Live Caption that metadata will be inserted into a text frame wherever to have decided you want it located. The problems for me are many. First, I do not normally have metadata in the files I use so the feature does not work at all and the choices are not available. Second, I commonly want to rewrite any captions I do have. Third, when i use captions, I have rules for how they are attached to the images, but often they move around depending on the image's position on the page. Live Caption cannot handle any of these issues. But for large shop, intense production situations like catalogs, product lists, and the like, I would certainly get this working and it would save an immense amount of time.

⌖ **Body heads:** These lesser subheads are now largely made irrelevant by the Character Styles palette and the ability to automatically produce run-in heads like used in this paragraph. As you see in this paragraph, nested styles using these character styles are often better than a small subhead in a separate line. But, for fancy type in an very graphic book, like this one, body heads are needed as an additional level of subheads.

9 Callout

Pull quotes or callouts are one of the more important typographic features in long articles and books.

As you can see above, they are type used as a graphic to recapture the reader's attention (in case it is wandering). They are usually related to the body copy instead of the heads. Occasionally they get extremely graphic, but the norm would probably be 50-100% larger than the body copy & italicized. They often use paragraph rules above and below to set them off. In this book, we also use a wavy rule with a gradient stroke if the occasion warrants. If they are actual quotes, it is a common device to make the quote marks extremely large (400 to 1,000% of the point size of the pull quote). By the way, the only difference between the two names is that pull quotes actually quote part of the surrounding copy.

Dealing with headers

These contain extremely important information to the readers. In reading importance, head and subheads rank just after captions and before lists. Headers are strong tools that provide almost all the impetus for a reader to start or keep reading the content. Don't forget, it is the content that matters. Heads let readers know how the content is progressing through an article or book. They are crucially important.

Turn off the hyphenation: In general, all headers have hyphenation turned off. In short paragraph styles like these, hyphens look very strange, to say the least (while maintaining politeness & political correctness).

Always Kern : Bad spacing is very obvious in larger type. It is true that the uneducated are not conscious of bad letterspacing. But subconsciously, something just does not look right and leads to trust issues with the content, the sponsors, and the author. In other words, readers will probably not notice other than to feel uneasy about the content—not good.

Always Break For Sense: It is critical to use soft returns (Shift+Return) to break heads between phrases. It cannot be emphasized enough how much difference this makes to readability. It is much more important than having all the lines the same length.

6 Headline

Large light heads

The impact is definitely lessened here in a sidebar with a tinted background but they still work.

If you have noticed in this book, we have gone with major heads that are a little larger than normal and that are a very light and open style. We think they contrast better in an extremely dense & busy book of this nature. *Do you agree?*

This is the most important, lead-in head for an article or chapter. It should only be used once. This needs a lot of contrast with the body copy – in size, color, and/or type style. Here is one of the places to use white space to break up the smooth grey of your type color and make the heads pop.

Typically the heads are sans serif and the body is serif, as you well know. However, heads should be a black sans serif and copy needs to be a book serif (lighter than medium, darker than light). The normal size for headlines is 24 to 36 point. The smaller the point size the bolder the type needs to be for the needed impact. In general, they should be reasonably short and pithy. In other words, they need to give the reader a clear idea of what is coming in the copy following.

Get up your nerve: The most common problem with new designers is not having enough nerve to use enough contrast between the heads and the body copy. Obviously it can be overdone. But, make sure there is enough contrast to compel your readers to read your heads. Print a proof and check.

The alignment needs to be closely watched:

The main thing is ease of reading and logical consistency. You need to have a plan and execute it with a set of well-designed paragraph and character styles.

⊕ **If the body copy is flush left:** the heads need to be flush left. If you try to center your heads over flush left copy the heads and subheads will typically look off center.

⊕ **If the body copy is justified:** the heads can be either left or centered.

⊕ **Flush right heads can be extremely dramatic:** BUT they are so far outside normality that they will disturb many readers. Understand your demographics before you get weird.

7 Subhead 1

This needs to be the same basic setup as the headline but about 25 to 33 percent smaller. Another option would be to stay at about the same size as the headline but go to a light or medium from the bold or black of the headline. The reverse is true also, with huge light heads and smaller very dark subheads. The main thing is simply to make sure that you control the contrast to help the reader make good decisions.

8 Subhead 2

This is smaller yet and almost always flush left (even if the heads and first level subheads are centered). Also if the 6 and 7 styles are black or extra bold, these second level subheads are often bold in the same font. These second level heads do not need nearly as much contrast as the larger, more important heads. As you can see, for this book we have reversed them out in white in a muted gradient bar.

o Kicker (A kicker is used to increase impact)

A specialized subhead of a head

This is a relatively unusual style it was originally developed (as far as I know) for newspapers. As you can see above, it is a little introductory subhead that leads into a larger subhead to help explain the header, add interest, and make the subhead more important. On a newspaper page with several articles the most important article is the one that get the kicker.

This is where readers tend to start reading. It's a surprisingly powerful tool of layout for complex documents with many articles.

Sidebar styles

There are no real rules here, but let's give it a shot. First of all, sidebars, by definition, contain peripheral information. In other words, they contain data that is interesting and nice to know; but they are often tangential to the main thoughts and concepts of the body copy. This means that they should be de-emphasized a little. We still want the body copy to be primary.

Tinted sidebars

The key to remember is that the tint in the tint box will mess up your type. Even at 150 linescreen, the tiny little dots will blur the edges of your characters. So you need to pick typestyles that will not be damaged by those dots. This is why we usually use sans serif for our sidebars. When coupled with the fact that our sidebars are usually very brief, this works well.

If your sidebars are going to be long, even a parallel story with your main body copy, maybe you should try something like Century Schoolbook or Acadami maybe even a strong contrast like **the slab serif fonts of Rockwell or Serif Gothic.** Because of the lessened contrast you can use much blacker type than normal. In some cases, an actual Black or Display weight printed at a 70% tint works well.

Sidebars are usually read only by the best readers

As far as type is concerned, you often want a font that contrasts with the body copy at least. Depending upon how you intend to use the sidebars, you may wish to pick typestyles that contrast with both the main body and its heads. As we mentioned earlier, in our books we try to set up our sidebar styles so we can use them for emphasis within the main copy also.

However, you'll do well to remember that sidebars are for entertainment—a reward for the good readers who are really enjoying the read you have produced for them. This means you can be a bit extreme here to good effect—**but keep it readable! ;-)**

Don't disregard them: sidebars are extremely powerful. Not only do they reward good readers, but they can greatly enliven the oayout and make the design of your book, newsletter, or magazine much more compelling. They through the page off center gracefully, adding asymmetrical interest to the visual presentation. Plus, they add white space and open up your composition. They're a good thing.

Objects
Anchored to Text

One of the nice things InDesign added several versions back is the ability to anchor an object to a location in the text. This makes it possible to have a graphic frame or a text frame floating next to a column of type that will move with the type. More than that, if you copy or cut the type and paste it in somewhere else the anchored object comes in along with the type in the column. If you cut the object itself, it keeps its anchored attributes.

 Very important tip: Once you have formatted an object as an anchored object, you can cut it and paste it in anywhere else in the type and it retains its anchored properties.

The dialog box you see to the right is confusing:

The good news is that you can simply turn on preview and make changes until you have what you want. The even better news is that these options are usually part of an Object style which we will cover next, and Preview works the same there.

You can see to the right that I have made my anchored object's align to the .75" margin in the gutter of this book. With a four inch column, it takes a book that is around 8" wide before the sidebar area is large enough to hold graphics of a reasonable size.

In the lower capture to the right, you can see the object is anchored

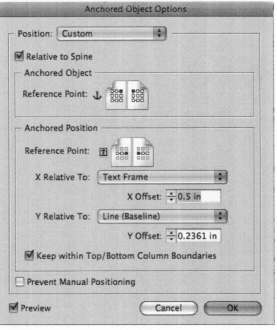

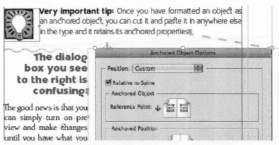

to the last character of the paragraph above it and its reference point is the upper left corner handle. It is set up to move that upper left corner handle a half inch outside the text frame toward the gutter of the book.

Position: Can be "Custom" or "Inline or Above Line". Custom gives you many options: a Relative to Spine checkbox, which proxy handle used to locate the position, and measured from which reference point in the text frame. We never use Inline or Above Line for some reason—just a personal style thing on our part.

Relative to spine: We are using this almost exclusively in this book. This way, if an anchored object is moved from the left page to the right page, the object changes sides. In this book, anchored objects are on the right on the left pages and on the left on the right pages. We wanted to keep the body copy to the outside edges of the book because it makes it easier to read and you do not have to break the spine of the book to do so (hopefully). This automates this choice.

Reference points: The top choice is for the handle of the object being anchored. The bottom choice is for the handle of the frame that contains the Anchored Object Character (AOC).

X offset relative to: The horizontal offset can be measured from the anchor marker, the text frame, the column edge, the page margin, or the page edge using your chosen reference point.

The Y offset relative to: The vertical measurement can be measured from the line (baseline, cap height, or top of leading), the text frame, the column edge, the page margin, or the page edge.

 When beginning, the measurements seem to defy logic: In most cases we find we have to adjust and readjust our anchored object settings to get what we want. That is one reason why we always add our anchored objects with an Object Style (which we will cover next). On practical level, we almost always have to move the objects after they are anchored. But they retain that new location without any issues.

We find the proxy handles are the key: The top set controls handle of the object used from where the distance measurements are made. The bottom set controls the other end of the offset measurement.

Keep within top/bottom of column boundaries: This moves the anchored frame up or down so it does not extend beyond the top or bottom of a column.

Prevent manual positioning: You can lock it up so the frame is exactly where you want and cannot be moved. However, we always want to massage the location—at least a little.

This does take some practice

There are at least three ways to add an anchored object to your page. The one we recommend as the best (the 3rd one in this little list) will be discussed at the end of the Object Styles section that follows this section on Anchored Objects. And we didn't even mention pasting in copy that already has an anchored object attached to it.

1. Inserting an object into an insertion point

This is the method that Adobe assumes you will be using. We do not recommend it because you have to set up every anchored object separately and because it demands many locally formatted adjustments to make it work. It does add several extra options.

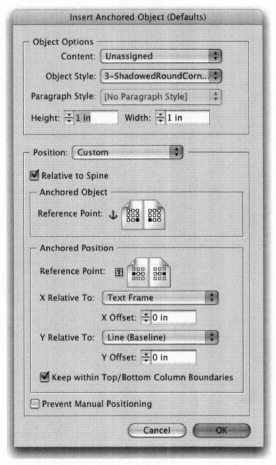

Content: You can choose the frame type: text, graphic, or unassigned. Of course, leaving it unassigned means you can use either option.

Object style: You can pick an Object Style to automatically be applied to the anchored object. As you will see in the next few pages, this enables us to preset these anchored object options and save it to a style.

Paragraph style: You can pick any paragraph style to be applied (which, of course, can include a nested character style).

Size: Height & width of the frame added. You use this to make an anchored object a specific size (leave these fields blank if you don't want the original size of the graphic changed).

The process is easy but a little complex. You use an insertion point in the text from which you want the object anchored. Then you choose Object>> Anchored Object>> Insert... . If you do this a lot you'll want to add a shortcut. An Invisible Anchored Object Character (AOC) is added at that point that looks like a Yen symbol (¥) in the color of your frame ¥Anchored Object Character. An empty frame will be added that is anchored to that location. You can then add type to the newly generated frame or place a graphic into that frame. The frame will be anchored to the insertion point and move with the type.

2. Converting an inline graphic

This is probably the easiest to understand. You place or paste a graphic into an insertion point – thereby creating an inline graphic. Then choose Object>> Anchored Object>> Options and follow the same procedure that we talked about in the first (Adobe-style) method. The options you set up in the Anchored Object dialog are applied to the selected graphic.

> **Note: it is much easier to select the inline graphic and apply an object style that converts the inline graphic to an anchored object. We'll cover that next. This book uses four object styles with anchored object options.**

3. Convert a graphic to an anchored object with an object style: and then cut it & paste it into an insertion point. It's almost like magic as the object just pops into position from the insertion point you choose.

As mentioned, we'll discuss this further in the Object Styles section that follows. This is the best method for many reasons.

 CONCEPT — Text wrap limitations: There is one foible of anchored objects. If you want to put a text wrap around the anchored object, it will only wrap text starting with the line below the anchored object marker. So, you regularly need to make sure you add the AOC marker to the line above where you want the text to wrap around the object. You can copy and paste the object by copying and pasting the AOC, but because it has no width it is tricky to select and move just that character. It is far easier to just select the anchored object itself, cut it, and then place an insertion point where you want to be anchored from—and paste.

Most people don't use anchored objects much as they begin their career – but use them increasingly as they gain experience.

Object styles

You can have styles for objects as well as text. This will enable you to more easily maintain a consistent look. In these new object styles, you can control everything found in the following panels:

- Paragraph Styles
- Stroke + Corners
- Text Frame Options
- Text Wrap
- Frame Fitting
- Anchored Objects
- Swatches
- Effects
- Story

So, you can set any of the Text Frame Options, turn on Optical Margin Alignment, Adjust the Frame Fitting options (in CS3 or better), and control the anchored object settings. You can make styles for text frames and for graphic frames. In addition, you can make any of the saved object styles into your default text frame style or default graphic frame style.

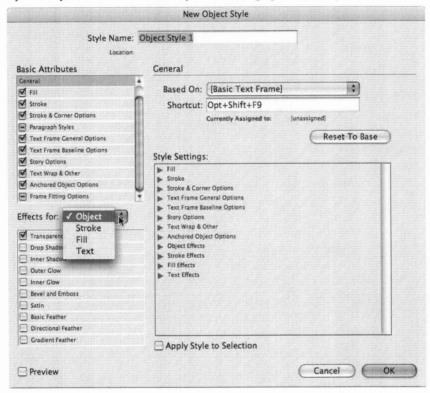

This Is One Of Those Options That Is So Complex It Takes A While To Get Used To: As you can see above, the dialog box is a bit complicated. But it will probably become one of your mainstays. Object styles may not seem to be as necessary as paragraph and character styles – but, they certainly help production speed once you have them set up—especially if you have a book like this that uses many graphics. At the end of this section we will cover why you really want to use an object style to make all of your anchored objects.

As in the paragraph and character styles, they give you global control of the look of your entire document. They really help with consistency of placed objects. Like with any style, if you edit a style every instance of use is changed. Of course object styles can be based on another style and all of the styles can be applied with shortcuts of your choosing.

We spent a year in 2005-2006 building training materials for a large corporation with a dozen subsidiaries scattered around the country with differing workflows. They were making a massive change from Quark 4.1 on a Mac to InDesign CS2 on a PC. We were constantly forced to implement the same radical revisions to the various sets of materials to customize them for the individual companies. Originally, we were not using anchored objects or object styles much at all. By the end of the process, we relied on them so heavily that all graphics were anchored in a styled frame (unless they were placed as a simple inline graphic).

Before adding this type of layout assistance to our workflow, it was taking several hours to rearrange pages, move pages from one document to another, move graphics, and so on. With object styles and anchored objects, we simply copied the type and the graphics that were anchored to the type moved in position automatically. Then we just used the "Copy Links To (Folder)" command in the Links palette option menu to move a copy of the graphics to the new document's folder and automatically fix the links. It was an amazing time saver of many hours for each set of documents! A single person, without help, was able to radically revise four-five pages and copy the changes to five or six other very different documents within a half day (because they all used the same sets of styles).

A default Object Style you really need

Adding anchored objects is a little tedious unless you have some object styles set up. One of the most painful aspects of making anchored frames to hold illustrations, sidebar notes, or headlines is the tediousness of the repetitive filling out of the anchored object dialog box. *The simple solution is to make those settings in an object style.* Then all you do is place the object and hit the shortcut to convert it to an anchored object and to offset it where you need it.

As we will discuss in the page layout chapter that follows, designing your columns and sidebar areas before you start laying out the document will save an immense amount of time. For example, you will quickly decide that your page size needs to be chosen so that you can implement anchored objects smoothly and fluently.

There is no way we can tell you how you are going to use object styles and anchored objects. All we can say is that you will use them a lot and that you need to make plans before you begin bringing in your copy and graphics if possible.

Make a new Object style with all the options turned off. Turn on Anchored Object and set it up like you see below. We gave it a shortcut of Command+Shift+Num1—this gives you a way to anchor objects and keep them aligned to the left edge of the text frame. We would also suggest you add an automatic text wrap of Jump Object.

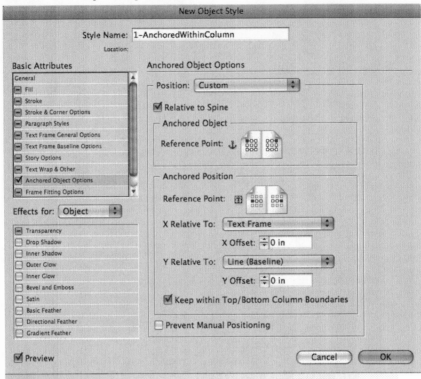

Once you have your anchored style set up the way you like, save the document you are working on. Then close all documents and go to the Object Styles palette (with no document open). Choose Load Object Styles... from the Option Menu and add the 1-Anchor style. From then on, all new documents will have this style available.

The butterfly to the right will move with the type, anchored to the paragraph. As you become used to the idea, you will use it more and more in your layouts.

The goal is to develop a set of paragraph, character, object, table, and cell styles that are available by default in all new documents you create.

New CS5 Features
to set up columns

Many of the new features for CS5 revolve around page layout. In a book like this that is primarily about styles, there is no need to mention things like the donut that appears in the center of a placed graphic that allows you instant access to the content of a frame. The same is true about the ability to rotate any placed graphic with the Selection tool.

But some of the things are part of our styles setups like the Split and Span column commands. And others just help us set up columns and grids, so I thought a brief coverage of the decisions that need to be made about page size and column usage would be appropriate.

Size

Often document size is a given. Book, magazine and newspaper sizes are determined by the publisher, for example. If you have any options, make sure that you design for an economical cut out of the paper stock you choose. If you come up with some really wild cuts or folds, check them out with your printer or bindery before you show them to your client. There are some terrific folds that have to be done by hand – but, handwork costs a fortune! A quick conversation with your bindery can save you lots of money and uncounted heartache. There are times when that custom hand-folded job is the perfect solution. Usually, forcing the bindery to do a lot of handwork is one of the quickest ways to a blown budget

On-Demand Choices: One of the things I've had to deal with as I have taken my writings on-demand is the limited sizes available. It seems like there are quite a few until you look at getting the books distributed. At that point, all the choices quickly resolve on 6" x 9". It's not a size I would choose if I had any choice, but to get this book distributed I'll do it. However, I will offer a square version on Lulu to satisfy the aesthetic side of me.

Margins

Again this seems to be too obvious, but many ruin their job here. The most common amateur mistake is to make margins too small. On digital printers, you need to be very careful to stay inside the maximum image area. You can assume that you need to leave .375" margins, minimum. On digital printers and presses, you often need to leave half-inch margins.

In addition, margins are often a large part of style. If you are trying for the elegant look of an old book, for example, you will need huge margins. There are many formulas, but here's one you can try: 100% top, 125% outside, 200% bottom, and 150% inside (for example, 1" top; 1.25" outside; 2" bottom; and 1.5" inside).

Conversely, if you need to convey cheap bargains – yard sale flyer, grocery store ad, and so forth – you need very small margins, gutters, and a lot of rules and boxes. You need to fill every open white space, making the page look like everything is crammed in to save money.

Readability: Margins have a lot to do with this for multi-page documents. For example, you want to make sure you leave enough gutter (the margin on the inside of the pages) to minimize the need to break the binding just to read the book. That is why I have 1.25" for the inside margin on this book with .75" the inside margin for the anchored objects. This is really the minimum, but it's about the best we can do with a 6x9 book.

Columns, layout adjustment, gridify, span, split

The new choices in CS5 make the decision about columns more difficult: There has always been a choice between text frames divided into columns and threaded text frames. For me this is a no-brainer. I like threaded text frames. The new Gridify feature makes this extremely easy to produce.

Gridify: As you drag out your text frame simply type the right arrow to add more columns and the left arrow for fewer columns. When you release the mouse, these column divisions result in dividing your marqueed area into evenly spaced multiple threaded text frames.

Live Distribute: The problem with gridify is that you do not have any control over the gutter between the threaded frames. This has been solved by another new feature. If the select all the new threaded frames, you can drag the side handle while holding down the Spacebar and the spacing between the columns can be adjusted. Obviously, this will take a little practice, but it is really quite slick and saves a lot of time.

Spanned headers: As mentioned, the most demanded feature for many years now has been the ability to have headlines and subheads span multiple columns. CS5 has that problem solved but only with text frames internally divided into columns. It works as expected and very easily. However, you are still going to have to use text frames that are internally divided into columns. The only way to do that easily is with an object style. You can set up an object style to add the internal columns necessary to any selected text frame.

Split columns: We covered this on pages 62 & 63. It also works well for those times when you want temporary column divisions within a column. TIP: If you change one of the paragraphs in a split column setup into a style that spans columns, the copy before that header will be divided above that header and the rest of the copy will be divided below that header. But that header will go across the entire original column.

Let's continue with tables

This is an area of page layout that has only been available for a few years. Throughout the '90s, there was no professional application to make tables. Many people just did them in Word and ignored the bad type, poor letterspacing, horrible controls, and so on. Now both Quark & InDesign have excellent table producing tools. InDesign's are better—with a larger feature set, but primarily because InDesign does better type.

InDesign Tables are part of type and edited with the Type tool

A table is a grid of text frames called cells: each cell acts much like a normal InDesign text frame.

You can insert inline graphics, use paragraph styles and character styles.

All selections are done with the type tool: The Type tool changes as it moves over different parts of a table, as you can see to the left. At the edges, it changes to a small bold arrow that lets you select a row, a column, or in the upper left corner the entire table.

Selector arrows

If you move your Type tool over the corner of the table you are working on, this arrow appears. If you click the mouse, you'll select the entire table.

Similar directional selector arrows appear vertically at the top of columns or horizontally at the left side of rows.

Tables can go from frame to frame: column to column and page to page. They flow like text in general with the small surprise that entire rows jump to the top of the next frame even if there is just barely not enough room.

You can have headers and footers with multiple rows of each if you like: When the table continues on the next frame, column, or page, a new set of headers and footers is generated.

Tables are separate from the rest of the text: In some ways they function like an inline graphic. In most ways they function like an interconnected group of text frames. There are a few limitations though.

1. You must make a text frame first: you cannot have a table as a separate object.

2. **Headers & footers can only be selected or edited in the first frame:** of a set of linked tables across frames, columns, &/or page.

3. **Page and column breaks can only happen between rows:** If you think about it, partial cells would be impossible to deal with.

4. **Shortcuts are often different:** Table has its own context in the Keyboard Shortcuts dialog. You can set shortcuts that only work in tables.

5. **Tables can extend outside the enclosing text frame:** In this way they function like an inline graphic. However, it can be hard to select type in the cells outside the text frame containing the table. You'll have to put your insertion point in a cell inside the enclosing text frame and then tab through to get to the cells outside the frame.

Table design

When setting type, there are times when rules, leaders, tabs, and columns are simply not enough. It can be argued (and Bringhurst does in his typography book) that anything more than simple tabs with no rules or leaders goes too far. That may have been true in the last century. But in this one –

He is wrong!

However, there is certainly a need for restraint. Too many rules, boxes, and borders imprison type and make it feel cheap. Sometimes cheap is what you need, but do it on purpose in that case. Especially in the case of tables you need to keep it light and easy to read.

Table & Cell Styles (CS3)

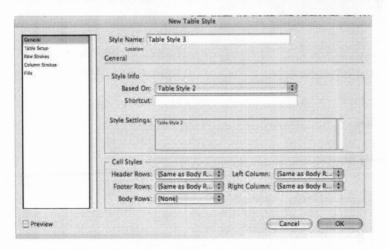

With InDesign CS3+ Adobe had taken the capabilities of Paragraph, Character, and Object styles and used them to create styles for that unique text object, Tables. You can do amazing things with tables once you become comfortable with them. We offer advanced tips & tricks for form design with tables in books on tables sold on the Radiqx Press Website.

Assuming that you are familiar with how styles work, Table & Cell styles still take a little preplanning. In CS3, we were continuously closing the New Table style dialog to go make a new cell style. Once there we had to close the new Cell Style dialog to create The paragraph styles necessary.

 Cell Styles come first: It is important that you set them up before you make your Table Styles—because—the first choices you make in a table style is which cell styles you are going to apply and where. Of course, in CS4, it is possible to add new cells styles inline.

 InDesign CS4 has added the ability to create new cell styles from within the New Table Style dialog box: There is a new entry in the list of existing styles to make a new cell style. This is a major new feature.

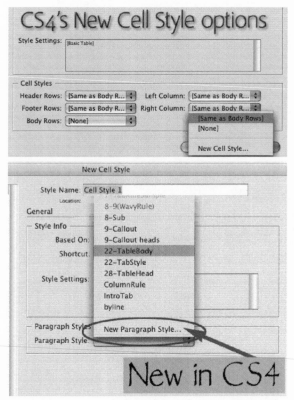

CS4's New Cell Style options

New in CS4

Cell Styles
(CHARACTER STYLES FOR TABLES)

Cell styles format selected cells in a table. You can control the paragraph style used, how the text is located within each cell, the stroke and fill of the cells, and the diagonal lines you might want to use. In the New Table Style dialog are separate choices for header rows, footer rows, the left column, the right column, and body rows

The only trick (in CS3) was to make sure that you have the paragraph style you need **before** you try to use it in a Cell style. If not you would have to close the new Cell Style box and open a new paragraph style box to make the style you need. CS4&5 have solved the problem.

Text page

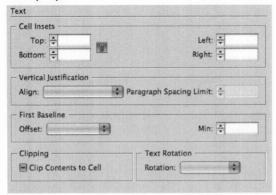

This page controls everything in the Text Frame Options dialog, plus the ability to do limited text rotation in 90° increments.

Strokes and Fills

This page allows you to set the stroke for each side of the cell with the normal choices of the Stroke panel. You click on the proxy lines to turn them on or off. Sadly, the colors you choose have to be in the Swatches panel before you start the process, or you'll have to quit and go create the new swatches necessary. Plus, if you use a gradient, you can't tint it. If you want those options like we do, go make a feature request at the Adobe site.

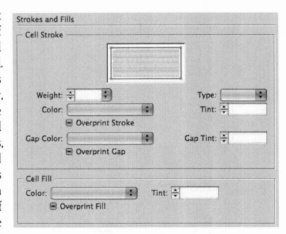

Diagonal lines

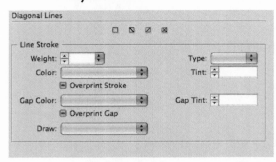

We assume some people somewhere use these. What else can we say?

To repeat, you need to set up all your Cell styles before you build your table styles: Actually, you don't but you'll waste a lot of time that way.

Table Styles

Table styles use all the controls for tables that you are familiar with plus you can apply cell styles to specific rows like the header rows, footer rows, left column, right column and body rows. This is where you set the overall table border and any alternating strokes or fills you might want. You can also set the space before & after the table here also.

Again the styles are very straight forward and use the same basic concepts and techniques as the text and object styles we have already covered. **But unless you have CS4 or CS5:** *you need to have the Cell Styles for those five categories set up before you create your table style.* Otherwise you'll have to quit out of the Table Style dialog to go back and make the Cell styles you need. This wastes time and is very frustrating. Of course, CS4 solves the problem.

Table Setup

Here you can set the border of the entire table, or that portion of the table shown in each frame, column, and page. Cell styles can override portions of this if you wish, because they are applied on top of the table style.

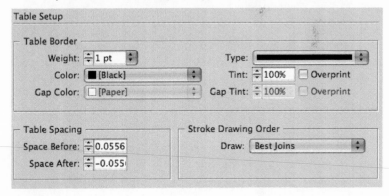

Table spacing: This is the only place you can control the space before and after a table. Even though a table seems to be in a paragraph, paragraph spacing will not control it.

Stroke drawing order: Best is good.

Row Strokes

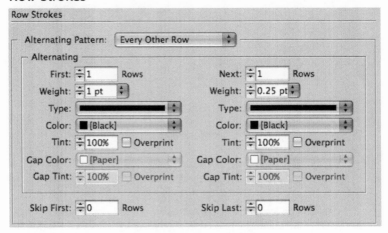

You have many options here: Every Other Row, Every Second Row, Every Third Row, or whatever Custom setup you can imagine with only two choices. Plus, you can skip x# of first rows or last rows.

Column Strokes

Here you have the same choices vertically.

Fills

You also have the same alternating choices for fills. The only limitation is that you have to choose whether you will use alternating rows or columns. You cannot do both. Shucks!

General guidance

The only real limitations are your sense of taste & style. However, remember the goal. Presenting written copy in a manner so that it is read. Like all things we do, if they notice the design they miss the content, in most cases. For tables, our suggestion is to supply the minimum necessary to enable unimpeded readability.

Building Forms

Now that you have table and cell styles you will probably be using tables more. However, one of the dirty little secrets of this industry is that tables are the best solution to one of most graphic designers' "worst projects". We're talking about forms – old-fashioned printed forms to be filled out with a pen or pencil. We put the quotes around that because they are one of our favorite projects as long as we do not have to do them full time.

Some simple rules & guidelines in form design

Always fill out the form yourself: If it bothers you, no one else will even bother to fill it out.

Find testers: Hopefully you can find members of the demographic you are trying to reach. But, equally important is to have a forms proofer who looks for inconsistencies, items missing, poor organization, lack of interior alignments, and so on.

Leave enough room: Think up the longest content you think will be used.

Use enough leading: The old hand-drawn forms used a 24-point leading as a minimum in most cases. That corresponds to a third of an inch (and often that seems cramped. If you leave too much space the writers will tend to write too large, but give them some breathing room at least.

Organize it logically: Simple things like having the home phone, work phone, cell phone, fax, and email in the same general area are often overlooked.

Ask for everything you need: We just finished a registration form where one of the critical pieces of data needed was the age of registrant — but they never told us that.

I spent a couple months consulting for Topform Data in Rio Rancho, New Mexico before I moved to Minnesota and they later hired one of my best students. They were an excellent company and treated their employees well. They had three full-time graphic designers. Much of their work was ridiculously complicated medical and dental forms – complicated by the fact that they were originally set up in FreeHand and had to be almost completely redone for InDesign. InDesign CS2 solved many of their problems with tables (though it was a radical change for them). Imagine if I'd had CS5 to show them.

You will be surprised at the number of times you need to design a form to be filled out by hand. *Do not just blow it off!* Forms design is good money and a real challenge. The largest problem with forms is that so few people actually fill them out. The stats are a little better for online forms that are submitted with a click of a button. However, for printed forms often only 10% to 25% of the forms printed actually get filled out. This is a similar problem to the readability issue for typography as a whole.

Making Forms Usable

How many times have you tried to fill out a form only to be stymied by rows of tiny boxes (for each letter) or a city line a quarter inch long and you have to write in Philadelphia? These are basic issues to be sure, and already mentioned. But they are often ignored by the designer who thinks he or she is oppressed & mistreated because they have to produce a form in the first place.

The exercise in the following pages assumes that you can learn how the various dialog boxes work in context — as you use them.

If you need more detailed instructions about the various commands and dialog boxes for making tables, and you are not satisfied with the help app that comes with the software (that's what we use), We highly recommend Sandee Cohen's Visual Quickstart for InDesign CS3 or CS4. We have it available in the bookstore on the Radiqx Press site for you.

http://www.radiqx.com/academy/bookstore.html

Dealing with existing forms

One of the most powerful uses of tables comes as the solution to one of the most difficult jobs in our daily work: duplicating existing forms with minor changes. Our clients become very attached to these old forms that they started using decades ago. The problem is that decades ago everything was done by hand so these forms often have features that are quite difficult to recreate digitally in software.

The best thing to do at this point is to show you a sample of a common old form (with the names changed to protect the innocent). As you will see, many things that

Customer's Order No.				Date	
Name					
Address					
Phone No.					
SOLD BY	CASH	C.O.D.	CHARGE	RETURN	PAID OUT
QUAN.	DESCRIPTION			PRICE	AMOUNT
				SUB TOTAL	
				TAX	
				TOTAL	

All claims and returned goods MUST be accompanied by this bill.

Rec'd by _____

THANK YOU

were simple to draw with technical pens are more difficult to produce with digital software. You will regularly have clients who love their old forms. You can make them very happy by giving them what they want in a new digital document. For more complex samples, see *More Complex Forms Samples To Reproduce* on:

http://www.radiqx.com/academy/training.html

Make grids into forms by merging

One of the common tasks we run across is the need to reproduce existing forms, with changes (of course). Here's a little procedure demo for a very simple example of this.

Getting Set up

Get referenced graphics here:

http://www.radiqx.com/academy/training.html

The form we are working with is available as a scan on the Radiqx Website called SimpleReceipt.jpg (URL is to the right). We are going to take this scan and use it as a background on top of which to build an exact copy. If you have a job where the duplication of orders is a normal part of your duties, this will revolutionize your workflow. If it is a large portion of your work, you know how much time can be spent trying to duplicate clients' existing forms.

Historical note: This type of form has been used for so many years by so many companies from so many suppliers that you may be asked to virtually duplicate it. Its design has become a comfort to customers. But only if you are going for nostalgia and old-fashioned ambiance. The font used has usually been Optima or a variant of it. The size might vary a little depending on the print supplier.

A single table form

You should read this with an eye to doing one of these projects on your own. Obviously, if any of us were designing this project from scratch, we would simplify the cell structure. However, we are not convinced that it would look as good to the customer. But for this demo let's just duplicate.

1. **Open new document in InDesign:**
   4" x 6.5" with 3/16" margins (.1875").
2. **Place the scan:** align it with the margins setting the bottom of the words THANK YOU at five-eighths inch (.625").
3. **Select the JPEG:** With the transparency panel make it 35% opaque. This grays it out to help you see the actual new table on top more clearly.

4. Open Layers Panel: Lock Layer 1 (with the JPEG in it). Make a new layer and move it on top. You can rename it &/or color it something better than the default garish red.

5. Make text frame: With the Type tool drag out a text frame that starts at just above the grid area and extends down below THANK YOU. *Normally, you would start the text box above the company name so you can enter the logo & name as needed. The entire page is in one text frame, but for this exercise we are ignoring the company name.*

6. Count rows and columns in grid: As you can see to the left, there are 18 different rows and eleven different columns. Count every vertical or horizontal line around a box or field as a separate column or row unless it lines up exactly.

7. Insert Table: Choose Table>> Insert Table... **[Command + Option + Shift + T]** and use 18 rows and 11 columns. Press **Enter**. The table will be added to your text frame.

8. Click in table with the Type tool to enable editing: Then use the diagonal arrow at the upper left corner of the table to select it all. Use the Stroke & Swatches panels to make the borders (stroke) .5 pt Black and make the type Optima or a variant like Zapf Humanist, 6-point .

9. Open Cell options: Press **[Command +**

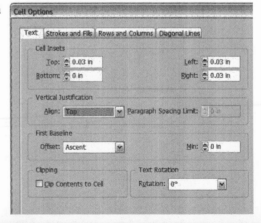

Option + B] and change the insets to .03 top, 0 bottom, .03 left, and .03 right. Set the alignment to top. You can see the settings to the right. Then press OK (or execute it with the Return key).

10. With everything still selected: Make all the type flush left. Yes, I know there is no type in the table yet. We are pre-formatting the table at this point. **Note:** *It greatly speeds up production to preformat cells before you add type wherever possible. Yes, we could set up Table & Cell Styles, but our assumption is that you will never have to do this look again.*

 Tip: If you have CS3 or CS4, it is better to set up a table style using cell styles with these settings. But for now, let's just go through this step by step as if you have never done this before and have no idea what to do next. For some of you this will be ridiculously easy. But please bear with us. Things do get much more complex.

11. Align the rows: With the selection tool, select the text frame and align the top left corner of the newly formatted table with the top left corner of the grid of the placed graphic. Then click in the table to activate the Type tool so you can edit the table. Starting with the second horizontal line in the grid, drag the grid lines down to line up with the scan. You see the results to the right.

12. Align the columns: in the same way, starting with the second vertical line from the left, drag the column dividers left and right until they line up with the vertical dividers of the scan. The result should look like what you see to the right. As you can see there are several extra vertical dividers because the original designer [lost in the mists of time] didn't bother to line things up better [or thought the slight misalignments were an asset].

13. Merge the cells: *Note: You will probably want to add a shortcut to your keyboard shortcuts if you have not already done so. Under the Tables Menu Product Area you'll find the Merge Cells command. There is no shortcut by default, we would suggest Command + Option + M or Ctrl + Alt + M with a Tables context.*
Now, with your type tool and looking at your sample, select cells that need to be merged and press the shortcut we added for Merge Cells or you can click on the Merge Cells button in the Table Control panel, or you can right-click and use the Merge Cells command in the contextual menu. The shortcut is by far the fastest method. So, if you were disobedient, go add the shortcut NOW. The process will look

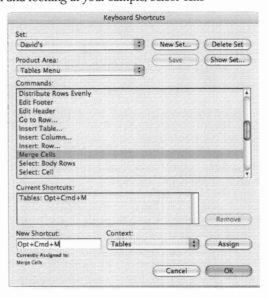

something like this as you merge the cells. The three cells below are selected and ready to merge. Those above have been merged already. Those below need to be done next until you have them all.

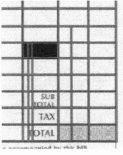

14. Merge all the cells that need merging: You will quickly see why you made the extra column divisions.

15. Add the type: As mentioned when we started this project, this form is almost always set in Optima demi-, semi-, or plain bold. In the digital age, there are several clones of the original like Zapf Humanist 601 and others. To modernize it, use Brinar. Click in a cell holding copy and type in the type seen in the scan. Most of the copy is 7-point, the grayed row in the middle is 5-point, SUB TOTAL, TAX, AND TOTAL are larger. Some of the cells are centered. Press **[Command+Shift+C/Ctrl+Shift+C]** to center the type.

Tip: It might seem easier to set up cell styles with these settings. But when you are **duplicating** a form, every single piece of type usually needs adjustment, so you would be locally formatting each cell regardless. It is easier to do it the way shown.

16. Add the type below the table: Click in the type above the table again to get outside the table. Hit the Down Arrow key twice and then hit Enter to start a new paragraph below the table.

Don't be in a great haste to charge your client for the time it takes on a simple piece like this. You'll probably be better off to save it in a folder called Forms templates or something equally original, for you will almost certainly sell this design to many clients in the future. It is now very easy and fast to change colors, copy , fonts, and so on. But including the scan, it only takes a half hour regardless.

For Rec'd by _____ you'll want to use a Shift+Tab to kick the rule to the right. It isn't worth the time to set up a leader in this case. The multiple below line rule characters will often need to be tracked together to make the line solid.

17. Add the gray to the tinted cells: select the tinted cells and open Swatches. Set the fill at 15% Black. You'll have to do this three times to color all the cells that need to be gray.

18. Delete the scan layer

It took much less time to duplicate the original form than it did to write about it

The time to do this simple form was around 15 minutes—and I'm a very slow typist. Typesetters doing this full-time can probably shave a minute or two off the time. The grid matches perfectly. The type needs a little kerning to be perfect. But, it is good to go as is [for most clients].

The good thing is that corrections are easy because the entire document is in one text frame. All the type is live and editable. The table is live and editable. A reorder would be a cinch to produce.

The final result looks like what you see on the next page

As we mentioned earlier in this chapter. There are two more samples to practice with on the Radiqx site, and complete instructions for reproducing them are found in *Adobe® InDesign® CS4: Styles & Forms*. This small 48 page book can be purchased from the Radiqx site or from Lulu.com if you wish to see the additional materials.

Using submitted word processing files

Yes, we know that this is very basic, known material for many of you. **If you know this stuff, skip to page 95.** But it is so important to production speed we are putting it in here as a review. Regrettably, it is often necessary to spend many minutes (if not hours) removing all the secretarial formatting before copy can be flowed into a page layout with any degree of freedom. We'll show you how in a bit.

The list of problems goes on for quite a while:

- ⊕ **Double spaces:** All the multiple spaces have to be deleted.

- ⊕ **Copy typed in all caps:** This is usually converted to C&lc.

- ⊕ **Using a tab for the first line indent**

- ⊕ **Centering headlines with multiple spaces**

- ⊕ **Using multiple tabs:** usually instead of hard or soft returns to go to the next paragraph in a bulleted list

- ⊕ **Bad lists:** Lining up each line in a bulleted list with a hard return at the end of the line then multiple spaces in the front of the next line in the paragraph

- ⊕ **Multiple returns**

- ⊕ **Extra Space characters:** at the beginning and end of paragraphs

Placed Word documents often have many strange character substitutions

You may find things like an Ö instead of " and Ó instead of " and many more. Often the Upper ASCII characters on a PC get scrambled when added to a Mac document.

There are others: but these will usually get you where you need to go. There is a complete pop-up list in Find/Change in InDesign. You might learn many of them if you are working in a fast production environment with a large quantity of different clients (like an art department in a printing company).

Dealing with secretarial copy

Many jobs will come with a disk containing the copy. For the moment we will assume that it is in a format you can read and import. Often though (unless all of your copy comes from in-house), the copy will have been input by a secretary with no training in printing requirements. It will be filled with multiple spaces and returns. Copy that should be italic will be underlined, or at the very least have quotes around it. The tabs will be made with multiple spaces. Centering will be done with the space bar. The list is almost endless.

You will have to eliminate all of these typos before you can format your copy. In the Find/Change dialog box, you will have to use a special code to search for and replace many of the invisible characters. InDesign uses a popup menu at the end of both the Find and the Change fields to add the special characters you need to fix. The list that follows is just an aid in memorization.

⊕ **^p is code to find or replace a hard return**

⊕ **^n is code to find or replace a soft return**

⊕ **^t is code to find or replace a tab**

Here is a procedure that will eliminate most common secretarial typos in a few brief steps:

1. Multiple spaces:
Use the find and change command to change all double spaces to single spaces. Just type in the space key twice in the find field and once in the change to field. Then click change all.

2. Multiple returns:
Use find and change command to change all double returns to single returns. **[^p^p to ^p]**. Then click change all.

Steps one, two, and three may have to be done several times: Many typists center headlines by using the space bar. This could use ten to thirty spaces. Each time you run the command, you will halve the number of spaces until there is only one left. The same is true of returns. Often spacing, or moving to the next page, is accomplished by adding many extra spaces or many extra returns. The same is true of tabs where complicated tabular materials are put together with the default half-inch tabs repeated as necessary to get things to line up.

In most cases you will also have to do the following steps to clean up your paragraph structure

3. Multiple tabs: Use find & change to eliminate all multiple tabs. In almost all cases these are used because typists usually do not set up tabs, they use the default half inch tabs and just use multiple tabs to clear things over far enough for their design comfort. **[^t^t to ^t]**. Then click change all

4. Eliminate spaces at the beginning and end of paragraphs: These are remnants of the multiple space, tab and return in steps 1–3 above. Use **[^pSpace**

to ^p] for spaces at the beginning & **[Space^p to ^p]** for space at the end. Then click change all

When you have the copy cleaned up, it is then necessary to eliminate all foreign formatting. Occasionally it is quicker to simply open the imported styles (they will have a small icon [a tiny floppy disc] at the end of the style instead of a shortcut) one by one and change the formatting within the imported style. However, this is usually false economy because all the based-on and next-style settings will be messed up (at the very least).

 There are times when it is quicker to work more directly with the foreign styles: In these cases, deleting each imported style and replacing it with the style of your choice works faster than steps 5–8. You may not need to eliminate all formatting in these cases.

5. Wipe out formatting: Select all to select the entire story. Then format everything to [Basic Paragraph].

Before you eliminate the formatting, make sure you print out hard copy: so you do not lose the location of bold, italic, and underlined copy. You will need to fix all of these things and eliminating all bad formatting will eliminate these errors as well—making them difficult to find or impossible, forcing you to start over.

6. Clear Overrides: With everything still selected, click on the Clear Overrides button in the Paragraph Control Panel. You can try holding down the Command+Shift keys as you click on the [Basic Paragraph] style – but this often does not get all the overrides.

7. Format everything to your basic body copy style: With everything still selected, format everything to body copy. This is why the style is called body copy, because the vast majority of the copy is set in this style. Doing this will enable faster reformatting because all that will have changed are the heads, subheads, and special paragraphs. Plus it will make your text as small as it will ever be to give you a clearer idea of how many pages you are going to need.

8. Using the shortcuts you have set up, format the entire job from front to back: If you have done it right, it should be a simple matter of holding down the Command (or Control on PC) key and typing Down Arrow, Style Number, Down Arrow, and so on.

This erases all foreign formatting

These procedures will eliminate all the foreign formatting (which is almost certainly littered with typestyles and fonts not found on your machine). In addition, the formatting that was used probably contrasts greatly with your approved layout. Word processors never format in multiple columns effectively, for one small example.

Now you are ready to format everything with your style palette. Edit your styles by eliminating all the imported styles from the palette. Often the fastest procedure is to eliminate all styles and then copy styles from a template you have set up properly.

Although this process may seem like a real hassle, it is much faster than anything else. Ideally, your copy will come in properly formatted. In reality, this rarely happens except with in-house copy or regular clients. Even then you often have to train them.

A general guideline is this: If the copy was not keyed in by a trained typesetting professional, all formatting probably should be eliminated before you go to work — simply to save you time.

 **Another thing that helps is to spell check in your word processor and in InDesign:** All spell checkers are a little different. Some catch initial caps on sentences, some catch double words, some catch transposed letters, some check proper names. All have a different set of features. So, the operative principle is spell check in your word processor, and then spell check again in InDesign after everything is formatted.

Why you want to make graphics in InDesign

One of the dirty little secrets in digital publishing in recent years is the fact that increasing numbers of designers are using InDesign for all of their graphic production. The primary reasons are the three we list below. However, another reason is that it is so easy to add pieces to an InDesign graphic from Photoshop, Illustrator, or FreeHand. All you have to do is a little set up.

True, InDesign is not an illustration program. However, it has several attributes that lead us to create most of our graphics within InDesign, adding pieces as needed from Illustrator and Photoshop. We have mentioned several of these abilities already, but they center around three basic capabilities.

1. **Typography:** Nothing else comes close. It is easier, in many cases, to do all your type in InDesign. Even when you are tearing type apart to make logos and graphics, InDesign is easier and faster than Illustrator in many cases. It can do many things with type that are impossible in Photoshop.

2. **Color control:** No other program has the color palette control of the Swatches panel in InDesign. We talked about this a little on pages 32 & 33.

3. **PDF generation:** InDesign simply produces the best PDFs. We use InDesign almost exclusively to make PDFs to be rasterized into high resolution JPEGs and PNGs for our clients. The InDesign file is much more editable and re-rasterizing it is quick & Easy

I do not expect all of you to immediately drop AI for InDesign. Nor do I expect you to forget about the bitmapped extravaganzas commonly developed in Photoshop. However, developing excellent type in InDesign and then rasterizing it in Photoshop will give you much better typographic control of your graphics.

Setting up Illustrator to produce pieces for InDesign

There are a couple of preferences you need to set and you can simply copy and paste editable paths from Illustrator. Many of Illustrator's fancy effects cannot remain editable when added to InDesign. However, extremely fancy drawings will work fine as long as there are no special effects. To restate things, plain paths work great even if they come from a source like a "watercolor brushstroke".

Set up for transferring editable paths

There are preferences in two applications that need to be set up in order to effectively use drag'n'drop.

✦ **In InDesign, on the Clipboard Handling page, make sure that Copy PDF to Clipboard is checked:** Illustrator can read that.

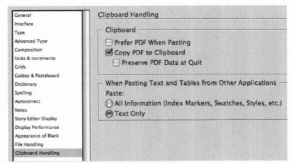

✦ **In Illustrator, on the File handling and Clipboard page, make sure that Copy as:** AICB (no transparency support) is checked. Under that, check Preserve Paths also.

This will set you up to be able to Copy/ Paste and drag'n'drop editable paths from InDesign to Illustrator and vice versa.

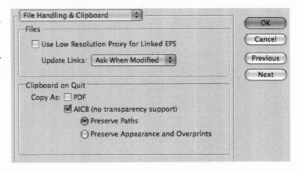

Setting up for Photoshop

With the above settings, you can copy/paste to Photoshop where you your choice of Pixels, Paths, or a new Shape Layer. We don't trust this process, however. We have always exported a PDF and then rasterized the PDF. We have no problems. So, try whatever you like but the PDF route is flawless.

Let's make a quick graphic

We'll start by creating a new document in InDesign that is five inches square. I will save that to a new folder. Into that folder I will place all the pieces used to make this graphic.

1. Place tiff in Illustrator & Live Trace

At this point, Illustrator finally traces bitmaps well enough to use. I have the scan of a large piece of calligraphy David drew years ago with a huge marker and saved as a TIFF. So, we place the TIFF into AI and use Object> Live Trace> Make and Expand. It does need a little clean up. We Ungroup and then delete the rectangle Illustrator produced from tracing the bounding box. Then we simply Select All, Copy, and Paste the paths into InDesign. In InDesign, we add a stroke and a gradient fill.

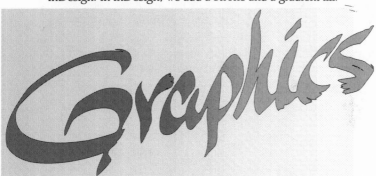

2. Add brushstroke oval from Illustrator

Illustrator is still the best with brushstrokes. So, we drew one in Illustrator. This does take a little work in Illustrator. First of all (like *@$# near everything in Illustrator) it needs to be expanded. Second, it needs to be ungrouped. Third, if you are in CS2 or CS3, the oval to which the brushstroke is attached must be deleted.

When that is done, we copy/pasted it into InDesign. We normally do this because InDesign's Swatches palette works so much more easily and gives us a lot more control. Also, subselecting paths in InDesign doesn't require the group select tool and all the clumsiness that brings. So, editing and adding the color was much easier than in Illustrator.

 Note: As an example of how easy it is. The brushstroke drops in as a group. I can simply click on any path with the Direct Selection tool to recolor it. Go back to the Selection tool to resize it. I simply took the tracing of Graphics apart and move some of the shapes in front of the brushstroke. When I released the compound path, the overall gradient remained. It was very fast and fluid.

3. Adding the text

The text was simply typed in. Once there I formatted it and placed it where it worked.

4. Readjust colors and layout

You do probably need to play around and adjust things. At least we do. But again that was very quick and easy, In this case, we added a half-dozen new gradient, on the fly. We resized and moved various pieces around. We adjusted the colors of the brushstroke so readability was damaged as little as possible.

5. Massaging the graphic

We made several little changes to finish things off. We finally decided that the oval was too heavy and missed our intention. So, we lowered the opacity. The final graphic does what we wanted it to do. It grabs your attention to make a point.

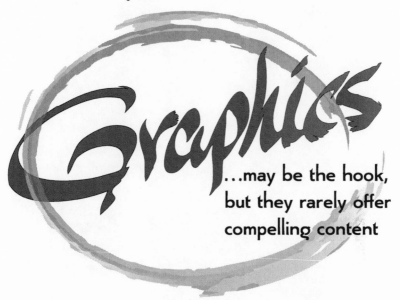

It's too bad the graphic has so little punch in grayscale. In full color, it was quite dramatic. Om the next page is another example of this type of thing done several years back for a magazine. You can see a brushstroke under the modified word Santa Fe. The brushstroke was done separately in Illustrator and colored in InDesign. Everything was done in InDesign other than the original brushstroke. In color, the words are saturated and sharply contrast with the dull brown adobe wall.

For another little exercise, let's quickly go through a simple tutorial we use in training. It's a silly exercise, but it should give you some ideas about graphics in InDesign.

**Open the door
to enchantment
in the
Land of
Enchantment**

You've never
had a vacation
until you've visited
Santa Fe.

Visit us at:

http://www.santafe.org

Getaway to the city different. A city that embraces its natural environment unlike any other in the United States. A city whose beautiful, brown adobe architecture blends with the high desert landscape. A city that is, at the same time, one of America's great art and culinary capitals. Whether you're planning a visit, a meeting or even a movie, Santa Fe welcomes you.

Damn the torpedoes

1. Open a new document:

Set size to 5"x5". Turn on document grid under View>> Show Document Grid

2. Draw circle:

Choose the ellipse tool. Holding down the Alt/Option and Shift keys draw a circle from the center out with a one inch radius. You could also draw any size ellipse and select it. Using the upper left proxy handle in the Control palette type in X:1, Y:2, W: 2, and H:2 Either one will give you a two-inch circle.

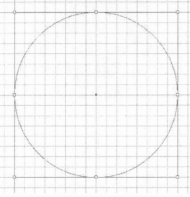

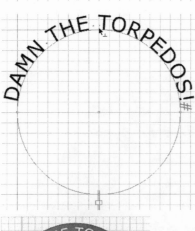

3. Place type on circle:

Choose the Type on a Path tool and click on the circular path. Type in the type, centered using the font of your choice, but make it beautiful. It would be good if you spelled torpedoes correctly. ;-)

4. Draw new circle:

Make this one the same way as the last one, but make it 2.5" centered around the first circle. Choose Object | Arrange | Send To Back. Make a radial gradient with the new Gradient Swatch command off the Swatches palette -- colors are your choice -- and fill the new circle. Add a half-point stroke of black. Select the type and color it something light.

5. Draw rectangle:

With the rectangle tool, draw a rectangle that is one inch tall and three inches wide. Fill it with a linear gradient of your choice. Use a stroke of None. Select the path with the Direct Selection tool. Using it and the Pen, as necessary, make the rectangle into a wave shape. We had to drag out the handles with the Convert Point tool and then click on the handles with the same tool to get the shape we wanted.

6. Copy shape to produce a path with the identical curve:

Next with the Alt/Option key held down, drag a copy of the rectangle down. Select the top two points of the rectangle with the Direct Selection tool and delete them. This will produce a path that matches the bottom of the rectangle. Don't worry about the fill because you are going to attach type to this new path. Then the fill will not show

7. Add type to the new path:

Select the Type On A Path tool. Click on the path with the tool. Type in Full speed ahead! In the font and color of your choice. Select the path with the Direct Selection tool and give it a stroke and fill of none. Select the path with

the Selection tool and mover the type up into position. Select the banner and change it to multiply mode in the Transparency palette. It should look something like this.

Yea, it's simple.

To make it better you probably should click on the transformation center of the circular torpedo phrase. Often that center is invisible to the naked eye, but it appears next to your cursor when you hover over it. By dragging that around the circle you can adjust the location of the type until both ends of it are the same distance above the banner.

OK! We could push it a little

But you get the idea. The basic point is: that for the simple drawing tools, they tend to be a bit better behaved in InDesign. Regardless, the Swatches panel is far superior, The PDFs are much better. And, the typography leaves Illustrator in the lurch.

Of course this is just our opinion!

As is this whole darned book...

We pray this has been helpful to you. Please write us if you have any comments or criticisms. You can also go to Chakham Lev's Radiqx Press FaceBook page to leave comments. He can always use a new friend.

http://www.facebook.com/radiqxpress

Made in the USA
Lexington, KY
08 September 2011